In the name of God, the Beneficent, the Merciful

The Daughters of Olive

*In the Memory of the Martyrdom-Seeking
Courageous Women of Palestine*

Compiled by: Muhammad Ali Samadi
Translated by: Kaneez Fatima Asad
Edited and annotated by: Abu Yahya al-Hussaini

Name of the book: The Daughters of Olive *"Dukhtarane Zaytoun"*, in the sacred memory of the brave martyrdom-seeking women of Palestine

Authors: Esmail Abdul-Latif al-Ashqar and Momen Muhammad Ghazi Bessissou

Compilation: Muhammad Ali Samadi

Translation: Kaneez Fatima Asad

Editing and Annotation: Abu Yahya al-Hussaini

Publisher: Jerrmein Abu Shahba

Year: 2019

ISBN: 978-1-7330284-3-1

"Palestinian women are routinely harassed, intimidated and abused by Israeli soldiers at checkpoints and gates...Women's health has suffered as a result of their inability to reach health centers. Pregnant women are vulnerable to long waits at checkpoints. ….. 55 Palestinian women have given birth at checkpoints and 33 newborns were stillborn at checkpoints, owing to delays or denial of permission to reach medical facilities."

Israeli military checkpoints and closure imposed over the Palestinian territories barred hundreds of pregnant women from receiving the needed medical checkups and tests during the course of pregnancy…..

Israel is responsible for the death of 33 newborn Palestinian babies, after soldiers banned the mothers, while laboring, from crossing military checkpoints on their way to hospitals…

(UNHCR, 2005)

Dedicated to

The Great Spirits of the Martyrs

Dr. Abdulaziz al-Rentissi,

Sheikh Ahmed Yaseen

and

The Daughters of Olive

Contents

Prologue

What you are reading is the third chapter of the book "Palestinian Woman in the range of a Zionist sniper", written by Esmail Abdul-Latif al-Ashqar and Momen Muhammad Ghazi Bessissou.

The sections on the martyrs 'Noora Jamal Shalhoub', 'Zainab 'Isa Abu-Salem' and Dalal Al-Mughrabi have been added to the original text after being compiled by the Research Department of Setad Pasdasht Nehzat Jahani Islami (Office for the Global Islamic Movement). This book, on the occasion of International Conference on *'Dukhtarane Zaytoon'* (The daughters of Olive), was translated by the Office for the Global Islamic Movement in the memory of the brave and self-sacrificing women martyred in Palestine and published with the cooperation of *Bonyade Shaheed wa Umour Issargaran* (Martyr Foundation).

We hope that all those who shared the effort for the printing of this book will have the blessing of these brave women martyrs, who are alive and whose pure spirits are in peace in the heavens and the dwellers of the earth owe their lives to their reviving martyrdom.

Looking forward for the day when Bayt al-Moqaddas[1], the Holy Kaa'ba and Karbala are set free.

Spring 2009

---

[1] Holy Jerusalem, the first Qibla of Muslims

Preface

On the 7th of December 1987, a Zionist driver deliberately ran over a group of Palestinian workers with a trailer, killing and severely injuring 13 Palestinians. This incident and the Zionist regime's humiliating negligence of this crime set ablaze the fire of the first uprising by the Palestinian nation against the occupiers of Bayt al-Muqaddas (Holy Jerusalem), the uprising which become known as Intifādā al-Oula[2]. In a period of less than 6 years, this movement became a horrible nightmare for the occupiers of Quds. The Zionist government, which in the 40 years of its existence had only faced the weak and coward Arab governments and small groups who carried out limited guerilla operations on the borders, was now, for the first time, facing an enormous uprising of people, people who were not carrying red flags with hammer and scythe nor with the signs of the Ba'ath movement or other nationalistic movements, but chanting slogans of '*Allahu Akbar*' (God is great) and carrying green flags with '*La ilā hā illā Allah, Muhammad ar-Rasul Allah*' (there is no God except Allah and Muhammad is the Prophet of Allah) written on them and coming out on the streets with stones and sometimes cold weapons, disturbing the fragile psychological well-being of the Zionists, who had gotten used to arrogance, and forced them to think of new ways to calm the situation.

The Oslo Peace Treaty between the Zionist invaders and the Palestinian Liberation Organization (PLO), with a promise of a Palestinian Government, apparently caused the Palestinian anger to cool down for a while. During the Intifādā al-Oula, only 383 Zionists were killed by the Palestinian defenders, compared with over 2000 Palestinians who were martyred.

---

[2]The first *Intifādā* (uprising)

The greatest achievement of the Intifādā al-Oula was the birth of various resistance organizations which were based on the Islamic ideology to challenge the Zionist regime. This had never happened in the history of Palestine and their struggle against the Zionists.

The massacre of people present for prayers in the 'Ibrahimi haram'[3], in the city of Al-Khalil[4] , by a Zionist extremist provided an opportunity for the newly-founded organizations such as Hamās[5] and Jihad-e-Islami[6] to take revenge of the blood of the innocent Palestinians from the Zionists, who were used to killing and being proud of their acts. The actual potential of such newly-founded groups, which most of their members were around 18 to 20 years old at beginning of the Intifādā al-Oula, was unknown until the 28th of September 2000. On this day, Ariel Sharon, the incarnation of the Zionist arrogance and extremism, walked into Bayt al-Muqaddas and caused the barrel of gunpowder, which had come into existence during the period of 7 years due to the humiliating and degrading acts of the Zionists and the so-called promises of peace and a Palestinian government by the Zionists, to explode and the fire of the Second Intifādā sparked in the heart of the Zionist regime.

In its beginning, this new uprising, which became known as the Intifādā al-Aqsā, was believed to be like Intifādā al-Oula

---

[3]*Al-Haram al-Ibrahimi* or Ibrahimi Mosque, the holy place attributed to six Prophets including Prophet Ibrahim (a).

[4]Al Khalil is a historic city in West Bank

[5]*Harakat al-Muqāwamat al-Islāmiyyah*, (Islamic Resistance Movement) was created in 1987 by Martyrs Sheikh Ahmed Yassin, Dr. Abdel Aziz al-Rantissi and Mohammad Taha of the Palestinian wing of Egypt's Muslim Brotherhood at the beginning of the First Intifādā.

[6]*Harakat al-Jihad al-Islāmi* (The Islamic Jihad Movement) or Palestinian Islamic Jihad was founded in 1979 by Dr. Fathi Shiqaqi. He was greatly inspired by Islamic Revolution of Iran and the personality of Imam Khomeini (ra). Dr. Fathi Shiqaqi was martyred by Zionist Mossad agents in Oct, 1995 in Malta.

and the Zionists aspired that they could suppress this rising as well with their fictitious diplomatic promises and an insignificant damage.

But the time and the location of this long-standing war had undergone serious changes. A few months before the Intifādā al-Aqsā, Palestinians had witnessed the first military defeat of the Zionists through the hands of Hizbollah and as a result, saw a different way and a new horizon in front of them. The enemy which seemed invincible had a weak point and the Palestinians aimed for it.

With the first martyrdom-seeking operation carried out by martyr Nabil Arair[7] on the 26th of October 2000, the number of these operations increased drastically until in 2003, the Israeli media publically announced that the security system of the Zionist regime is on the brink of a massive ruin. Barukh Kimerling, an Israeli sociologist, writes in his book 'The Political Destruction': "If the youth with stones are the symbol of the Intifādā al-Oula, then, the symbol of the al-Aqsā Intifādā, for both sides, are the suicide bombers." This time, the damage done was to such an extent that the Zionist regime pulled back unconditionally. It seems that with the pull-out of the Zionist regime from the Gaza Strip in 2005, the al-Aqsā Intifādā, will also vanish but the future definitely holds events that are unpredictable. During the 5 years of the second uprising, the number of the Zionists killed and injured reached 11,000. And what is surprising is that more than half of these casualties were caused by the martyrdom-seeking operations carried out by the Palestinians. In order to realize the depth of the devastation which the Zionists have faced because of these martyrdom-seekers, the best evidence

---

[7]Martyr Nabil Arair, 24 yrs old pious young man from Gaza city, was a primary school administrator and belonged to The Islamic Jihad Movement (*Jihad-e-Islami*).

comes from General Evi Dikhter, the head of the Israeli National Security (Shabak). He said, in an interview with the Israeli newspaper 'Haaretz' (9th of August 2004): "Since the beginning of the Intifādā in September 2000 until 8th of August 2004, the number of the Israelis injured and killed is much greater than it is since the establishment of the Israeli government in 1948 until the year 2000 because in the 4 years of the Intifādā, 11,356 Israelis have been injured and killed compared to only 4319 in the time period of 1948 – 2000."

What you will read in this short compilation is a brief review of the lives and the martyrdom of ten martyrdom-seekers out of 350 who carried out operations in the occupied Palestine. Indeed, it can be boldly claimed that the qualities and characteristics of these eight heavenly women are the symbol of all the martyrdom-seekers of the land of olives during the years of Intifādā the martyred men and women which not only Palestine but the whole of the Islamic world, will be proud of, in this world and in the hereafter.

With the hope of the liberty of Quds and Karbala,
Muhammad Ali Samadi

Message of Ayatollah Hussein Nouri Hamadāni

On the occasion of honoring Palestinian martyrdom-seeking women

"Those who are fought against are permitted (to fight) because they have been wronged, and Allah is indeed able to help them" [Qur'an, 22:39]

The history of none of the nations of the world is as dark and black as the history of the Zionists and among the records of all the criminals of the world, there exist no records more shameful than those of the Zionists and no authentic document has described their crimes and atrocities like the Holy Qur'an has. From the point of view of the Holy Qur'an, Zionists are a group of people whose actions and traits in the history have been rejecting and rebelling against the signs of God, denying and killing His prophets, slandering and insulting the believers and the chaste ones, having cruel hearts, unfaithfulness, distorting the book of God, distorting the truth and reality, greed and an intense love for the materialistic life, groundless claims, stubbornness and enmity and better to say it in one word, that is having all the aims against humanity and fulfilling them by means of force, conspiracies, breaking promises, standing against peacemakers and disturbing the security and tranquility. God, the Exalted, has described their behavior towards the Prophets in this verse of Qur'an:

"Certainly, We gave Moses the Book and followed him with the apostles, and We gave Jesus, the son of Mary, manifest proofs and confirmed him with the Holy Spirit. Is it not that whenever an apostle brought you that which was not to your liking, you would act arrogantly; so you would impugn a group [of them], and slay a[nother] group?" [Qur'an, 2:87]

We already know that it is more than fifty years since the arrogant powers of England and the United States America created the Zionist government to preclude the spread of Islam and to have its strategic headquarter in the Middle East. Zionists, for achieving this goal, rendered the Palestinians homeless and through deceit, treachery, massacres and crimes, removed the Palestinians from their own homes and farms and never abstain from any atrocity against the Palestinians. In all of these years, the heroic nation of Palestine and all the Muslims have been in a war against the Zionists but because of the support of the superpowers, specially USA, Israel has always been superior and powerful and Muslims have always been weak and defeated. In all these years, the heads of the Islamic governments accepted the Israeli government and indulged into conspiracies to preserve their positions and material benefits and as a result, gave away the dignity and honor of the Islamic nations until the Palestinian nation chose the way of "martyrdom-seeking operations" to struggle and defend their rights. The noble way was called as "suicide bombing" by the Arabs, who see everything with the eye of materialism and worldly gains. But Muslims, by adhering to the Islamic ideology, sincerely and faithfully chose the martyrdom-seeking operations as a form of Jihad and martyrdom in the way of God.

The world has witnessed that the Shi'as of the south of Lebanon, who by relying on martyrdom-seeking operations, finally succeeded in defeating and throwing the Zionist army out of the Lebanese land in the year 2000. It was for the first time in the history of the Zionist regime that the Zionist army was defeated. Following this, with the start of the second Intifādā the martyrdom-seeking operations of the Palestinian youth shocked the fully armed Zionists and took away sleep from their eyes and peace from their minds and their supporters, the dwellers of the White House, and traced a dark and dreary future for them.

Independence seeking and Islamic enthusiasm in the heroic land of Palestine has reached to such lofty heights that a mother, after sending her four kids for martyrdom-seeking operations, chooses the same for herself and attacks the enemy so that every piece of her body would cry out loud to the world for an innocent and homeless nation.

And at last, it is the martyrdom-seeking Jihad that has frustrated the Zionist regime. According to the Zionist statistics, 80% of the damage done to the Zionist regime during the Intifādā al-Aqsā has been due to these martyrdom-seeking operations.

What is more surprising and amazing is the fact that among these martyrdom-seekers, there are girls and a 22-year old mother of two children.

These martyrdom-seeking operations form a golden page in the book of the history of the Islamic Jihad and a black spot on the foreheads of those who see the Zionist atrocities and injustice but choose to stay silent.

It is indeed a pity to see some ignorant deceivers and liars who call these courageous actions "terrorism" and condemn them. They cannot see the reality of this sacrifice and faith for defeating the enemies of Islam and upholding the dignity of mankind.

The famous personality of the present times, the brave idol-breaker, the sage jurisprudent, the courageous orator like his ancestor Haider-e-Karrar[8] with the eloquence of his words

---

[8] Imam Ali (a)

reminiscent of the sermons of Imam Ali (a.s) in *Nahjul Balagha*[9], and the writer, the ink of whose pen is superior to the blood of martyrs and the freedom-fighter who was the symbol for thousands of freedom fighters to come and the one who was struggling for all the oppressed of the world, Imam Khomeini (ra) called martyrdom-seeking operation, a wise way of Jihad.

Therefore, since the oppressed nation of Palestine - the land which is the heart of Islam and belongs to all the Muslims – is facing the sophisticatedly armed Israeli army which is supported by arrogant powers such as USA and its allies and has no choice except Intifādā and carrying out martyrdom-seeking operations, their martyrdom-seeking operations are a form of Jihad in the way of God and the martyrs of this sacred path will be blessed by God.

"Do not suppose those who were slain in the way of Allah to be dead; rather they are living and provided for near their Lord" [Qur'an, 3:169]

The memorial and the honoring of martyrs, especially the virtuous women who, with martyrdom-seeking operations, courageously preferred a death through martyrdom over living without dignity under the dominance of an arrogant rule, is a radiant glory. These female martyrs are the pride of Islam and their holy Jihad is astonishing and their will testaments are praise worthy.

Hossein Nouri Hamadāni
21st April, 2005

---

[9]The most authentic compilation of sermons, letters and sayings of Imam Ali (a). Available at http://www.al-islam.org/nahj/

The role of women in martyrdom-seeking operations

When Intifādā al-Aqsā began, it was far from imagination of one's mind that it can acquire such an importance and reach such high dimensions. However, the passage of time showed that the Intifādā opened new ways and strategies to fight and struggle against the Zionist enemy.

One of the evident peculiarities of Intifādā is the prevalent participation of women in martyrdom-seeking operations, a phenomenon which had never been witnessed in the history of the wars between the nations of the world, let alone in the history of the Palestinian struggle.

The present text, through an analysis of the role of women in martyrdom-seeking operations, will try to look at and review the different dimensions of this topic.

Martyrdom-seeking operation and its legitimacy

The first subject that is set forth in the discussion of the role of women in martyrdom-seeking operations is the legitimacy of the action of carrying out martyrdom-seeking operations itself. In other words, the first question that comes to the mind is that does Islam give the permission of such action and is it counted as a permissible act in the law of religion? Normally, it is one's legitimate right to defend his life, property and reputation and this right belongs to every person or society and reason also directs that a person should take all the measures and try as hard as he can to defend his life and to obtain what is his legal right.

Islam also has a positive view of this matter and defending one's self in an Islamic society is considered lawful. Many religious authorities in Iran and in the Arab world have made comments regarding this subject.

1. Ayatollah Fazel Lankarani: "The martyrdom-seeking operations, if permitted by the concerned Intifādā officials and fitting all the conditions, are allowed and the whole world must know that the Palestinian people will make use of this way to fight this regime and to let the world hear the cry of the oppressed. Therefore such actions which defend one and one's country are lawful and the person carrying out such operation is considered a *shaheed* (martyr)."

2. Sheikh 'Akrameh Sabri, the Mufti of Palestine: "The one who is offering his life does not need any permission from here and there. We have to emphasize on the lawfulness of resistance and we don't have the right to stand up against Intifādā and Jihad but we have a duty to be at their side and appreciate them."

3. Sheikh Nasr Farid Wasel, the Mufti of Egypt: "The martyrdom-seeking operations carried out in the occupied Palestine by the Palestinian youth to eliminate oppression and to defend themselves, their homeland, their principles and their children and the Holy Islamic sites, are considered lawful."

4. Sheikh Mahmoud 'Ashour, Religious Authority: "Islam believes that whenever the land and belongings of Muslims are trespassed, it is an obligation for all the Muslims to rise for Jihad. Islam doesn't prohibit women from participating in martyrdom-seeking operations but validates it."

5. Sheikh Hamed al-Bitawi, Secretary of the Association of the Ulema in Palestine, has also confirmed the legitimacy of the martyrdom-seeking operations and the participation of women in them.

Considering the above statements, it can be said that carrying out martyrdom-seeking operations is lawful and has been validated by Islam and there is no difference between men and women regarding it. In addition to what has just been mentioned, there is another element that plays an important role and these are the thoughts of the Palestinians themselves about these operations and their support for it and this is the main factor that determines the continuation or the halt of these operations.

Many polls have been carried out regarding the martyrdom-seeking operations and the majority supports these operations. According to an opinion poll carried out by Palestinian Association for Cultural Exchange, 70% of the Palestinian population supports martyrdom-seeking operations while only 24% are against them.

An analysis of the role of women in martyrdom-seeking operations

In analyses regarding the function and role of women in martyrdom-seeking operations, the topic can be looked at from two different perspectives:

A. Analysis of the direct role of women in these operations.

B. The indirect role of women, which lays the foundation and provides the motivation for these kinds of operations.

A. The direct role of women

Regarding their direct role, the Palestinian women are side by side with the men on the warfront of the fight against the Zionist occupiers. If the Palestinian men see it as a duty to defend their land against the occupiers, then the Palestinian women have the same share in their sense of duty towards their homeland. The humiliating Zionist politics and the Zionist pressure are not limited to just Palestinian men but women are placed under even greater pressures and face even more difficulties. It should be noted that even before Intifādā, women had been playing a key role but it had been limited. An example is the act of Layla Khaled, a member of Popular Front for the Liberation of Palestine, in hijacking an Israeli airplane in 1969. The difference between the acts of women before and after the Intifādā can be described as follows:

1. Before Intifādā, the participation of women was very limited.
2. Before Intifādā, there was not much room for women for participation and activity. However, today the participation of women is approved by most of the Palestinians.
3. The women have welcomed this way of struggle (martyrdom-seeking operations) and their participation is highly distinguished.

The large number of such operations shows that it is becoming popular among the Palestinians and illustrates some points:

1. The age of all the female participants in these kinds of operations is below 30. With Palestine being occupied for the last 55 years and the propaganda of the Zionist regime to make the Palestinians forget the past and with some conspiratorial negotiations since 1990, the impression among the Israeli officials was that the new Palestinian generation is not willing to continue their forefathers' struggle. The commencement of Intifādā al-Aqsā and its continuation have rendered

the Israeli measures and conspiracies useless and the participation of women, especially the involvement of the young women and their presence on the warfront has led to the continuance of the struggle for the Palestinians' rights.

2. The majority of martyrdom-seeking women are from the lands occupied in 1967. This shows that the severe and humiliating policies of the Zionists and the deprivations, insults and degradation which the Palestinian women face every day provokes them to carrying out martyrdom-seeking operations.

3. A majority of the martyrdom-seeking operations have taken place in the lands occupied in 1948 and this shows the ability of the Palestinian women to pass all the security checkpoints and barriers placed by the Zionists; this has resulted in not even a single safe place for the settlers and this illustrates the incapability of the Zionist officials. A very important feature of martyrdom-seeking operations is their sudden occurrence and the Zionists, who are equipped with numerous spying devices, have not been able to stop these actions from being carried out by the Palestinian women.

4. Another subject is the great damage done to the Israelis as a consequence of these operations even though some of these operations were detected and stopped by the Israelis before they were carried out. But most of them were successfully carried out and showed that these kinds of operations are very useful for the continuation of resistance. The damage done by the operations carried out by women is more than the other operations.

B. The indirect role of women

It can be said that the indirect role of women is greater and more widespread and important than their direct role. And so, the cost paid for this role is greater, for example, a woman was arrested for supporting a martyrdom-seeking operation and was condemned to hundreds of years in jail by the unjust Zionist court and this lady is still living in the hard conditions of the Zionist prison. The reason for this is that there is a variety of things that women can do indirectly. Women who want to carry out martyrdom-seeking operations must take special military training and so there are a limited number of women who can get involved. On the other hand, there are a large number of women who can participate in the indirect struggle. Apparently, this type of struggle has no direct connection with the martyrdom-seeking operations but this struggle lays the foundation of the martyrdom-seeking operations. According to statistics, around 5000 Palestinian women have been arrested by the Zionist regime since 1967. Most of these arrests have taken place between 1968 and 1976 and then during the first Intifādā Even during the Intifādā al-Aqsā, more than 100 Palestinian women were arrested and most of them are still in the Zionist prison.

Another important discussion is on the educational role of the Palestinian women in bringing up their children and encouraging them to carry out martyrdom-seeking operations. Obviously, a youth brought up by a Palestinian mother, who is fighting against the enemy, will be able to carry out a martyrdom-seeking operation. Even the strength and feelings of these mothers after their children's martyrdom is exemplary. Umm Nidal[10], the mother of

---

[10]Her real name is Maryam Mohammad Yousuf Farhat. She is popularly known as Umm Nidal, or "the mother of struggle" and is one of *Hamās'* most popular candidates elected in the Palestinian legislative election, 2006. She sent three of her six sons on *Hamās* suicide missions against Zionist regime.

Muhammad Farhat who was martyred in a martyrdom-seeking operation, says: "Jihad is a religious command. We must teach this to our children. I sacrificed my son as a part of my dedication. I had always encouraged my sons to get martyred."

Another interesting story is of the wife of Marwan Barghouti[11], the general secretary of Fatah in the Western Bank and a prisoner sentenced to life in prison in Israel. She says: "We have no choice but to rise and to be firm. This struggle is for freedom and we must be victorious."

Standing up against the aggressors has its own costs; one of them is giving up life. According to the statistics, since the Intifādā al-Aqsā until the compilation of this work, more than 700 girls and women have been martyred by the occupiers.

Based on this, it can be said that martyrdom, imprisonment, offering the beloved ones for martyrdom-seeking operations, demolition of houses and... are the factors that reveal the importance and the role of women. All of the above mentioned hardships have caused immense pressures and suffering on the Palestinian women and the Palestinian women have tolerated all of these hardships with dignity, honor and resistance.

The outcomes of martyrdom-seeking operations carried out by women

Besides all the effects of the martyrdom-seeking operations and the crisis in Israel, these acts also have other consequences and some of them are mentioned here:

---

[11]Marwan Barghouti was Secretary-General of Fatah in the West Bank. He played important role in first and second *Intifādā* and is currently serving 5 life sentences in Israeli prison for leading attacks carried out by the *al-Aqsā* Martyrs' Brigades on Israeli soldiers.

1. Creation and Nurturing of high ideals: The first effect and reaction of these operations is the establishment of a new culture and its propagation in the Islamic societies. Palestinian women, by carrying out martyrdom-seeking operations, have created new ideals and models for Muslim women to follow. They have showed that if men had the main role on the warfront, then women can also have a greatly effective and impressive role on the front line.

2. Psychological effects: Normally in the western societies, it is not reasonable to accept that people should do anything to defend their beliefs and homeland. The martyrdom-seeking operations are not very well-received by the western standards of reason. The ability of the Palestinian women to efficiently carry out martyrdom-seeking operations has had a deep effect on the Western and Israeli societies and has made it clear for the Zionists that even the Palestinian women, and not just Palestinian men, are a danger to them. This is in a situation when the news in the occupied lands indicates that the continuation of Intifādā is adding daily to the dissatisfaction of the Zionist army and some Zionists have refused to serve in the army. The presence of fearless and courageous Palestinian women in the scene is what the Zionist soldiers did not expect.

The statistics reveal that the damage done by the martyrdom-seeking operations of the Palestinians has been enormous and that the Israelis now feel insecure, since from the beginning of Intifādā al-Aqsā till its fourth year, more than 1000 Israelis were killed. Definitely, the increase in the number of Israelis killed and a corresponding increase in the number of martyrdom-seeking operations has led to a great effect on the thoughts and opinions of the Israeli public.

3. The Zionist regime's incapability in face of the martyrdom-seeking operations: The martyrdom-seeking operations, as the best choice of resistance, have changed the balance in the favor of the Palestinians. The Zionist regime, equipped with the best military, defense and information facilities in the region, has not been able to cope with the martyrdom-seeking operations. The remarkable ability of the Palestinian women to carry out martyrdom-seeking operations by using appropriate clothing has struck the Zionist regime with a big blow and has forced the Zionist regime to fight back by using different policies. Some of them are listed below:

1. Destruction of the houses of those involved in a martyrdom-seeking operation.
2. Expelling the relatives of the person who committed the martyrdom-seeking operation from the occupied lands.
3. Creation of the Apartheid wall.
4. Israel's Foreign Ministry has been trying to approve an international law according to which a person who has committed a martyrdom-seeking operation is counted as a war criminal.

And of course, these policies have not had any significant outcomes for the Zionist regime in combating the martyrdom-seeking operations but they show the Zionist regime's helplessness and desperation regarding these operations.

4. Important consequences of the upholding of the spirit of resistance and Jihad among the Palestinians: When women have such kind of presence in the battlefield, the men are motivated to a greater extent and see their responsibilities clearly. The high spirit of resistance among the Palestinians shows that all the actions taken against them by the Zionists to degrade them have been unsuccessful and actually have increased their resistance. The presence of kids, youth, women, girls and men is a great evidence to prove this claim. It must be said that the Zionist policies have had an opposite effect and have turned against the interests of the Zionists themselves. As the spirit of resistance is increasing among the Palestinians, the Israeli society is being shrouded by a sense of hopelessness and disappointment. According to an opinion poll by Yadaout Ahrnout[12], 73% of the Israelis believe that Israel has lost its war against the Palestinians.

Conclusion

In the conclusion, it must be said that the role of women in the Intifādā, especially in the martyrdom-seeking operations, is greater and more important than the role of men. Their economical role as the manager of the house and their activities in the society, their educational role as mothers bringing up children and transferring the spirit of resistance and struggle to them, along with their role in martyrdom-seeking operations have blessed them with a unique and special status in the society.

These operations convey some important messages:
1. The extensive popularity of martyrdom-seeking operations and the involvement of women in them illustrate the injustice and oppression that the Palestinians are going through. The difficulties do not leave any other choice for the Palestinians but to sacrifice their lives.
2. The martyrdom-seeking operations are an indication of the failure of political tactics and conspiratorial negotiations.
3. With 55 years of occupying Palestinian land and trying to give it a legitimate color, Israel has taken many measures

---

[12]Israeli Newspaper

on the regional and international level, but all them have failed due to the martyrdom-seeking operations and their continuation.

4. Martyrdom-seeking operations are giving the Palestinians the most advantage over their enemy; therefore this opportunity cannot be lost. This is the only way of struggle that Israel does not have the ability to react to and control it.

Prelude

With the start of the year 2002, the Palestinian resistance witnessed a great turning point on its sacred path. This resistance, during the Al-Aqsā Intifādā[13], was blessed with the precious and dear blood and saw the rubble of demolished houses and lands and an endless hatred and animosity towards the Zionist regime and their atrocities.

The cruelty and crimes of Zionists are impossible to describe. A volcano should have erupted so that the outpouring lava would collect a little bit of the sufferings of the Palestinian nation since the beginning until today to make the Zionist enemy taste it.

The presence of women on the front line of struggle against the occupiers has been one of the great manifestations of this volcanic explosion; in a way that today, there is no difference witnessed between man and woman for Jihad and the path of resistance is not just restricted to men but men and women are united in confronting the ruling occupier without any differences.

At the beginning, the presence of women on the path of resistance was less but it increased day by day with great strength and manifestation. The devotion, self-sacrifice and presence on the scene of struggle have considerably increased and to such an extent that women, with their profound

---

[13]The second *Intifādā* which began in September 2000.

presence, have been able to find a dignified position for themselves in the very depths of the movement for the liberation and independence of the revolutionary nation of Palestine. The martyrdom-seeking operations that the Palestinian women have carried out are the best indication of the appearance of women in this historical movement for freedom.

In this book, we will present to you the stories of martyrdom-seeking women. Those who made their presence in the golden pages of the Palestinian history, conquered the peaks of resistance and struggle, and astonished the world with their sacrifice and, in this sensitive and important period of the Palestinian existence, became the legends with their amazing devotion and sacrifice.

Martyr Wafā' Al Idrees

Date of Martyrdom: January 27, 2002

The Palestinian nation had just started the year 2002, the days which were full of the crimes and atrocities of the Zionist invaders and their terrorist policies. The first month of that year, in which the Palestinian nation had seen the worst oppression and misery, had not yet finished when Islam and the whole world was a witness to a powerful bolt of lightning which defeated the terrifying wall and broke the dreadful silence and took away the darkness of night that had cast a shadow upon the problem of Palestine.

On the 27th of January of the same year, the Palestinian – Zionist conflict became violent than ever before and prophesied a new phase of struggle of the Palestinians against their Zionist occupiers, who devastated the lives of Palestinian people and their land and its Holy sites.

Wafā' Al Idrees was the first woman to enter the battlefield and, with a bomb, head towards the occupied territories of her homeland which consist of Quds, Yafa, Haifa, 'Aka, 'Asqalan and other cities that were occupied in 1948, territories which were heavily protected by advanced security measures, walls, obstacles and the Zionist army patrols so that no freedom-lover or dignity-seeker can find the opportunity to enter those lands and pay the Zionist regime back for all the massacres, crimes and terrorism.

In this Holy and purified land (especially the western part and Yafa), Wafā Idrees, while expecting the most beautiful moment of her life and with a bomb that she had placed inside her briefcase, courageously entered a Zionist commercial area to carry out an explosion that would shake the whole area and disturb the lives of the Zionists in a way never done before.

No one knew or even imagined that Wafā's flesh and bones would one day commingle and her purified existence would be the means of the burning of the aggressive occupiers and the parts of her purified body would be scattered in different directions away from her home, family, and friends.

What followed this martyrdom-seeking operation was ambiguity since the identity of the one who carried it out and those who had planned it was not known. For three consecutive days, no one claimed the responsibility of this operation.

Both the Palestinian and the Zionist sources persisted that Wafā's aim was not to carry out a martyrdom-seeking operation and blow her up. The Zionist police's detectives also questioned the operation's being martyrdom-seeking and described her intention as only placing the bomb in the chosen place and then abandoning it. Similarly, it was suggested that the bomb that was carried by Wafā had exploded before reaching the planned location or that there was a technical fault in the timer of the bomb which led to an untimely explosion or that the timer was not activated on purpose. There was no written document or any other pictorial evidence (which is common among martyrdom-seekers) that would confirm Wafā's intention of carrying out a martyrdom-seeking operation. Her family and relatives confirmed that they, while saying good-bye to her, had not seen any signs that would indicate that Wafā is leaving forever. Wafā had not told anything regarding this to her family. Likewise, one of the leading figures of the Fatah movement in Ramallah, who was in connection with this martyr, considered it very improbable that this operation was martyrdom-seeking and that Wafā's intention was to carry out a martyrdom-seeking operation. All the mentioned points strengthened the proposition that Wafā had the intention of giving the bomb to a man who would conceal the bomb somewhere or carry out the martyrdom-seeking operation himself.

All of these problems and propositions lessen the importance of the role of this female Palestinian martyr; but they cannot deny the damage and results of her struggle.

It was only a few moments after the explosion had occurred, and the number of the Zionists killed and injured was soaring. One Zionist was immediately declared dead and more than a hundred were injured.

Based on this and despite all the ambiguities and ifs and buts, Wafā succeeded in robbing the other women of the title of the first martyrdom-seeker woman and registered her name as the first one to open the door of martyrdom-seeking operations on women in the history of Palestine. Wafā, with this operation, became ahead of the other women, who showed bravery and courage and were martyred, because she entered an operation in which there was nothing awaiting her but martyrdom.

Wafā, who had passed her 26th spring in Al-Am'ari[14] refugee camp in Ramallah, was not a special or someone unlike the rest of the Palestinians, especially the Palestinian women; because what these women witness everyday doesn't leave them any choice but places them in one way and that is the way of resistance. But she was ahead of all the young women and those women who are keen on entering the battlefield and struggling and fighting with arms and being among the martyrdom-seekers.

Wafā Idrees finished her primary and secondary schooling in the schools of the camp and continued with her university education in the nursing school of the An-Najah National University in Nablus so that later on she would voluntarily start working for the Red Crescent as an officer for helping the wounded Palestinians, who face the Zionist atrocities in their most horrid and the worst forms.

She, while the treating and nursing of the injured oppressed people – that happened continuously and on daily basis, did not have the strength to endure and touch the dozens of life-threatening wounds and scattered bodies and to wipe the tears of the Palestinian children and to support and aid the injured elderly anymore. In her heart a holy fire was set ablaze. Only a huge explosion that would tremble the ground under the feet of the Zionists, could extinguish this fire.

The promised day on which the operation was supposed to be carried out, Wafā, after taking permission for a personal work from her workplace, left it and walked towards the

---

[14]Al-Am'ari refugee camp is located just outside Ramallah, in the territories occupied by Israel in 1967. It is home of over 11,000 Palestinian refugees. Zionist forces frequently break into this camp and destroy houses, take hostages and kill innocent.

Quds Avenue located next to the 'Al-Manara' square in Ramallah and hired a taxi for the occupied Quds and reached the 'Yafa' street, one of the busiest streets of the western Quds and one of most crowded spots of the Zionists, and arrived at the place of her heavenly ascension…

Wafā had disappeared for the first time in her life and when the Palestinian security networks informed her brothers of her disappearance, they did not believe it and thought that she would return home in a few hours but this wait continued for three days and there was no hope left for her family. Until Khalil, her eldest brother, who was working for the Palestinian security, informed his superiors of the disappearance of his sister. He was not aware of her sister's involvement in any armed struggle activities or her interest in a martyrdom-seeking operation. Blood samples were then taken from Wafā's brothers and sent to the Zionist territories for tests and inquiry.

In the afternoon of the 30th of January 2002, the four brothers of Wafā along with their mother who had been recently discharged from the hospital and crying for the disappearance of her daughter, were gathered together in their house when the house-bell rang and the truth about Wafā was exposed like a thunder bolt on their heads. The Zionist officials after matching the blood samples of Wafā's brothers with the one from the scattered body of this martyred lady were convinced that Wafā Idrees had been the one who had carried out the martyrdom-seeking operation in Yafa.

All the family members were astonished and dead silence took over the place until broken by the cry of the mother who was painfully asking her daughter to return home.

This atmosphere of surprise and shock did not last for a very long time and the family members were in charge of their emotions and were proud of Wafā's act. The mother of this martyr, in her interviews with the media, was very proud of her daughter because of her courageous confrontation with the occupiers and indicated that all the relatives and neighbors were very proud of Wafā's courageous act.

The Al-Aqsā Martyrs' Brigades - the military branch of the Fatah Movement -claimed the responsibility of this operation. However, the family of this martyr and some of her neighbors said that as far as they know, Wafā has not been a member of any Palestinian movement. E'temad Abu Labdeh, a very close friend of Wafā who was with her in the social activities of the community of women in Al-Am'ari refugee camp for 14 years, said with a trembling voice: "This was the only thing I did not think of. It was a long time since Wafā had been telling me, "I wish they would sacrifice me for my homeland". But I wouldn't understand the meaning of her words. She used to repeat these words frequently before this operation."

Without any doubt, the unawareness of even the people closest to Wafā of her plans and aims shows Wafā's remarkable secrecy. Apart from all the discussions that arose after the operation about her intentions on carrying out a martyrdom-seeking operation, the greatness of this act and its value as well as Wafā's passing all the obstacles placed by the Zionists to overcome and control resistance, caused the Palestine resistance to enter a new era and brought about a new and striking change in the Palestinian resistance. This new change was very valuable because it was going to be followed by remarkable consequences and outcomes due to a foundation of a new way and others' devotion to it.

Martyr Noura Jamal Shalhoub

Date of Martyrdom: February 24, 2002

Noura Jamal Shalhoub was a 16 year old student and was a daughter of a veterinarian. She was born in a religious family. She was distinguished for being clever with a high memory since childhood. She was adored at the school by all her classmates and teachers, and whoever got to know her, liked her. She was devoted to Islam and always had her hijab. She had memorized the Holy Qur'an by heart and in spite of her young age, she participated in many Islamic activities in school.

Noura was very sensitive towards Intifādā, especially Al-Aqsā Intifādā. She was greatly impressed by the life of the martyrs and collected the pictures and testaments of martyred leaders and martyrdom-seekers of Intifādā.

According to the persons close to her, she was greatly touched by the martyrdom of Mahmoud Abu-Hanoud[15], the commander of al-Qassām Brigades[16].

Whoever knew her was aware that she is highly informed of political and cultural affairs. She carefully followed the Palestinian and the world affairs and was aware of the conspiratorial peace negotiations regarding Palestine. In fact, what made her older than her age was her love for studying and following up the news from the media.

Not much is published about Noura Jamal Shalhoub, may be because she was very young. The only souvenir left from her is a picture which is not very clear and a testament, the contents of which show Noura's maturity and awareness. On 25th of February 2002, at the checkpoint[17] of 'Tayba' (the border point which separates the lands occupied in 1967 from the lands occupied in 1948), Noura carried out a martyrdom-seeking operation. The Zionists never mentioned the real damage and casualties done by this operation. The remains of her body were handed to her family after 2 days. Many people attended and demonstrated in her funeral procession. Noura's name was recorded as Palestine's youngest martyrdom-seeker. May God bless her great spirit.

The Will Testament of Martyr Noura to her Teachers and Classmates

---

[15]Mahmoud Abu-Hanoud was commander of Izz ad-Din al-Qassām Brigades in Nablus, West Bank. He was martyred by Israeli helicopter rockets on November 21, 2001.

[16]The Izz ad-Din al-Qassām Brigades, named after Martyr Izz ad-Din al-Qassām, (shortened to al-Qassām Brigades) is the military wing of *Hamās*. It was created in 1992 mainly under the direction of Martyr Yahya Ayyash.

[17]Israeli checkpoints crippled the daily life of Palestinians. Hundreds of patients have died waiting for hours to cross these checkpoints while on their way to hospitals or clinics. Over 80 Palestinian pregnant women gave birth at these checkpoints while 39 infants and 6 women have died.

"In the name of God, the Compassionate, the Merciful"

My dear sisters and friends, I want you to study well and respect your teachers, since they are like our mothers. I hope that when you get married, by the will of God, you will educate your children in the path of religion so that they would stand bravely against the tyrant enemy. In the end, I want you to pray that God will accept my martyrdom as well as those of others. I am grateful to all of my teachers and I am not able to express the respect I hold for them in my heart in this writing. God willing, I will enter the paradise along with them; since they have been suffering a lot for their children, family and the school. My dear teachers! May God bless you with a great reward and alleviate your sufferings. Dear teachers, if you have seen disobedience from me that might have bothered you, please do forgive me and God is greater than to be described and all praise belongs to Him.

May Islam and Muslims be victorious and shame be upon spies and killers!

Alive martyr, Noura Jamal Shalhoub

The Will Testament of Martyrdom-Seeker Noura Jamal Muhammad Shalhoub

I testify that there is no God but Allah, and Muhammad is His servant and messenger.

"In the name of God, the Compassionate, the Merciful"

"Fight all the polytheists, just as they fight you all, and know that Allah is with the Godwary." [Qur'an, 9:36]

This terrorist enemy has been imposing its aggression on my nation. Oh tyrant invaders! The time has come for me to teach you a decisive lesson. At the time of this operation, I have decided to send a letter to these invaders and tell them Oh Jews! You will not have any security in our land; get out of our land since this land is *harām* (forbidden) on you.

I have decided, with the permission of God, to attack these tyrants in this cursed blockade (Tayba checkpoint) so that they would know that they do not have security in my land. I am dedicating this operation to the spirits of the great martyrs: Fauz Badran, Amer Hozayri, Mahmoud Madani, Yasser Badwi, Raed Karami, Dr. Sabet Sabet, Faris Jaber, Mahmoud Abu-Hanoud, Nasser Hamdān abd-Ar-Rahmān Hamad, the martyrs of the massacre of Nablus and the martyrs massacred in Bayt Laham[18], Bayt Rima[19] and 'Ayn al-Fariah[20] and all the martyrs. And also to the families of martyrs and to those who are injured and to those who have suffered damage.

May Islam and Muslims be victorious! Down with the betrayers, spies and those who have murdered the *mujahidins* (resistance fighters).
Long live liberated Palestine
Noura Jamal Shalhoub

---

[18]Also known as Bethlehem. It is a historic Palestinian city in the central West Bank, approximately 10 kilometers (6 miles) south of Jerusalem.
[19]Bayt Rima is a district of Ramallah in West Bank.
[20]'Ayn al-Fariah is an important junction in the city of Nablus.

Martyr Dāreen Muhammad Abu-Aisheh

Date of Martyrdom: February 27, 2002

She is a unique model for young women to follow, a believer and a mujahida[21], who sold her soul to God and was satisfied to make a bridge out of her corpse for the rising Palestinian resistance and a flaming fire for revenging the enemies of God, religion and humanity which are at the zenith of tyranny and aggression.

She is a rare example for an aspiration which had come out of disappointment and despair, a model of persistence of youth who does not know how to give up and a model with iron will which does not allow defeat and weakness within and satisfies only when moved up for the sake of God.

She was an incarnation of a firm pledge and a determined oath to God, the Exalted, and devotion to religion and beliefs, who sacrificed her life for the sake of God.

---

[21]Female resistance fighter

This martyred mujahida is no one except 22-year old Dāreen Muhammad Abu-Aisheh, who was living in Bayt Wazn[22] in Nablus, in a family with eight girls, two boys and the parents. She was studying in the faculty of English literature of the An-Najah National University[23] and she was honored to be a martyr in the last year before her graduation.

Her life was like any other believer who is sincere and independent toward her Creator and devoted to all the aspects of religion. Her good behavior made her dear to her friends, neighbors and all of those who knew her.

Dāreen, since entering the An-Najah National University in Nablus – a university from where many of the *mujahidins*, combatants and martyrdom-seekers are educated - was active, full of energy and joy and was a member of Islamic association. This membership kept her aware of her country's problems and the sufferings of her nation. This awareness developed a volcano of anger and hatred inside her and she was always looking for the right time and place to direct its lava and fireballs at the Zionists, the invaders of her land.

With the start of Al-Aqsā Intifādā, which was followed by the flood of pure blood and massacres and tortures of the innocent, Dāreen realized that the promised time has arrived for her to show her hatred and take revenge from the occupiers and to embrace martyrdom.

With every day passing, the love of martyrdom was increasing in her heart and manifesting itself as the light of

---

[22]Bayt Wazn is a village located near Nablus in the north of the West Bank.
[23]An-Najah National University is a Palestinian non-governmental public university. It is located in the mountainous region of the northern West Bank in and around the city of Nablus. The university has over 16,500 students and 300 professors in 19 faculties. It is one of the largest Palestinian universities.

justice and freedom. The suffering that her nation was tolerating caused her patience to end. She could not witness the daily presence of bulldozers demolishing the houses of innocent people and destroying their future, dreams and hopes and forcing them to either surrender to the Zionist injustice or to leave their homeland.

Dāreen, in this situation, did not wait for somebody to come and help her people or assume that fighting the enemy is the responsibility of men. And instead of choosing the easiest and the least dangerous way which is to surrender, she decided, with an iron will, to rise for the victory of the children of her nation and carry out an admirable act.

Dāreen was capable of doing other jobs which were particular for women in serving their country, such as being a teacher or a social helper, helping the families of martyrs and those whose husband, brother or father is in prison, sending help without getting involved in the combat or play other important roles but she was ambitious with a strong will to reach the Exalted in perfection.

She had decided to break the walls of what was a tradition and take an important step further in her life and reach her valuable wish.

After reaching this stage of perfection, she was indifferent to her own worldly cravings and forgot her fantasies and her education although she was successful and could have graduated the same year. She had something else in her mind and could make it come true and nothing could stop her. She was constantly visiting the martyrs' family, sharing their sorrow and pain. Dāreen had participated in the funeral of many martyrs and she would never get tired of talking about the martyrs.

Dāreen was always thinking of her great dream and the noble wish of her life. She did not doubt it for a second. She once visited Sheikh Jamāl Mansour[24], one of the Hamās leaders, who was martyred by the Zionists in July 2001. But Sheikh Mansour did not allow her to go for a martyrdom-seeking operation.

Sheikh Jamāl Mansour's answer did not change her mind and she stayed faithful to her oath. Without giving up, she started looking for someone to guide her and make her wish come true.

Political analysts in contact with Hamās explained the reason of Sheikh Mansour's refusal to accept Dāreen's request. They said that he was a member of political movement of Hamās' office and that this office was not in contact with the branch of Hamās which is in charge of military and martyrdom-seeking operations and it was not that Sheikh was against this act.

After the passage of the first year of Intifādā and the beginning of the new year of the Palestinian-Zionist confrontation, Dāreen was still looking for a way to fulfill her wish until the news agencies announced the news of the first martyrdom-seeking operation carried out by a woman on the 27th of January 2002 and it was broadcasted that Wafā Idrees has carried out a martyrdom-seeking operation in the heart of western Quds. This news made her wish of martyrdom more ardent than ever, and she was certain that she is more closer to her wish than ever, and a path has been opened to make her wish, which was imprisoned in her chest for days and nights, come true. She was lost and found herself in the Al-

---

[24]Jamal Mansour, a senior *Hamās* leader from West Bank, and his brother, Omar Mansour, were martyred by Israeli helicopter gunships on July 31, 2001.

Aqsā Martyrs Brigades which welcomed her action of martyrdom-seeking operation and provided the explosives and the other necessary tools for the act. And although she was a member of Hamās, she did not consider it necessary to get their permission.

The martyrdom-seeking operation by Wafā Idrees was carried out on the 27th of January 2002. It was decided that Dāreen would carry out the martyrdom-seeking operation on the 27th of the next month (February) in one of the Zionist police stations in Yafa which is located in the lands occupied in 1948.

Everything essential was ready, from the explosive belt to the people who were responsible for taking Dāreen to the site of the operation. The promised time had come and Dāreen was entering a new stage in her life which was truly unique.

This stage can be described in one sentence: the phase of life with God and away from all the materialistic and worldly pleasures. Dāreen's mother says: "My daughter was up the night of her martyrdom, reciting the Holy Qur'an until dawn." Dāreen was a religious person who would pray, fast and stay up many nights reciting the Holy Qur'an but on the night of her martyrdom she was praying more than she had prayed ever before.

In that perfumed morning, which was the most beautiful morning of her life, Dāreen left the house with the explosive belt around her and along with two other Palestinian combatants, rode to the place of the action. The closer they were getting to the site of the operation, the greater was the number of the security check points and obstacles. This made it hard for Dāreen and her partners and they thought that they would not be able to carry out the holy action. It was as if the Zionist security forces were on alert and had the news that a martyrdom-seeking action is going to take place.

They had to make it through. It was somewhere in the half of the way when they were surrounded by the Zionist patrol cars. They were worried about their plan and the car carrying Dāreen and her two partners was stopped at the checkpoint of 'Mekabel', located at some distance from Tel Aviv. The Zionists wanted to inspect the car and its riders. The two companions of Dāreen, named 'Hafez Maqbel' and 'Moussa Hasouneh', came down quickly and showed their identification cards and announced to the soldiers that the third rider is their sister and that they are on their way home. The soldiers insisted on interrogating her. Dāreen stepped out and went toward the soldiers pretending as if she wants to show her ID but as soon as she was close enough to them she pressed the button of the explosives she was carrying and she...

Both of her partners were injured and arrested by the Zionist soldiers. The Zionist regime aanounced that 3 soldiers were injured. Dāreen's mother, 'Wafiqeh Abu-Aisheh', describes the last hours which she had spent with her daughter as, "She left without saying goodbye. I did not notice anything unusual in her behavior. The only thing I remember is that on Wednesday, the day of her martyrdom, she entered the house at noon and said, "What a nice food with a wonderful smell, you are a good cook" but she did not eat any of that food since she was fasting."

Later, when the relatives came to her house to say their condolences, Dāreen's mother said, "Dāreen was very sensitive to what was happening around her and when she heard the news of the pregnant women on their way to hospital being shot by the Zionists, she started to cry and wished that she could take revenge from the enemy."

She added, "Few hours before the operation, Dāreen called the house and said that she is in a place from where it's very difficult to get out. I felt she has an intention of doing something. The heart of a mother does not lie and I could tell that her patience had ended and if it had gone on like this, she wouldn't value her life."

Ebtesām, Dāreen's sister, recalls the last moments she had spent with her sister as, "When Dāreen left the house, she said, "I am going to buy a book." She returned after a few hours. Then, she again left the house but I did not know where she was going. She called us at 10:00 p.m. and said, "Don't worry, if God wills, I'll return. Put your faith in God. I'll be with you in the morning." These were the last words me and my mother heard from her."

Ebtesām is pointing to the fact that her sister had made an oath, which was to chop the Zionist soldiers into pieces, and had sworn to carry out a martyrdom-seeking operation against the Zionists who shoot pregnant women[25]. She adds, "When a young man in the village of 'Zawātā', which is near the place where we live, was martyred a few days before Dāreen's martyrdom, Dāreen went to visit the family of that martyr and blessed her handkerchief with the blood of that young martyr and made an oath that she would take revenge."

Ebtesām disappointedly says, "Dāreen was not a member of the Fatah Movement or the Al-Aqsā Martyrs' Brigades. She

---

[25]Several Palestinian pregnant women have been shot by Zionist soldiers at these checkpoints. In order to mentally torture Palestinian women, Zionist soldiers wear T Shirts written with: 'Kill Pregnant Women, 1 shot kills 2'.

was one of the most active members of the Students' Islamic Association of Hamās at the An-Najah National University. When Hamās did not accept her wish, she, because of her intense love for martyrdom, did not wait. And when she found out that the Al-Aqsā Martyrs' Brigadess has agreed to fulfill her wish, she did not hesitate and she joined willingly to get ready for the holy action."

After the martyrdom of Dāreen, her family published a picture of her wearing a green headband, on which the slogan of Hamās was written, holding a knife and looking ready for martyrdom.

From the very first moment of the broadcasting of the news of Dāreen's martyr, pride and delight could be witnessed in the family of Abu-Aisheh. The Abu-Aisheh family is very religious and well known for its struggle for the Palestinian cause because two of its members had carried out similar martyrdom-seeking operations before Dāreen.

On the 25th of January 2002, Dāreen's cousin, named Sofoof Abu-Aisheh, carried out a martyrdom-seeking operation at an old bus stop in Tel Aviv and killed and injured many Zionists.

Few days later, 'Omar Hafez', another one of her cousins, carried out a martyrdom-seeking operation near the city of Mihoula in the Al-Aghwar[26] district and left a deep scar on the body of the Zionist regime.

Dāreen gave up her life for the sake of God, religion, beliefs and nation and this was the fruit of her pure soul. She showed that the responsibility of the battlefield is not on the

---

[26] Al-Aghwar and Jericho Governorate of the Palestinian territory is located in the West Bank, north west of Quds (Jerusalem).

shoulders of men only; but women can carry out more sincere acts. Her name was added as the second martyrdom-seeking woman in the list of the martyrdom-seeking women during Al-Aqsā Intifādā and the reality testifies that she was one of those who were seeking martyrdom and an eternal existence and did everything they could do to make that wish come true.

The spirit of Dāreen Abu-Aisheh is alive among the people of her village and in the hearts of the Palestinians and she will be remembered for her kindheartedness, politeness, strong will, pure intentions and her help to her nation. She is like a peak of a high and firm mountain. She was just a young woman, but her action testifies that she was worth a thousand men, but even more.

The Will Testament of Dāreen Abu-Aisheh

In the name of Allah, the Beneficent, the Merciful

Peace and Praise be upon the Leader of the *mujahidins*, Our
Prophet Muhammad (s).

God, the Exalted, says in the Holy Qur'an, *"Then their Lord answered them, 'I do not waste the work of any worker among you, whether male or female; you are all on the same footing. So those who migrated and were expelled from their homes, and were tormented in my way, and those who fought and were killed – I will surely absolve them of their misdeeds and I will admit them into gardens with streams running in them, as a reward from Allah, and Allah – with Him is the best of rewards.'"* [Qur'an, 3: 195]

Since the status and repute of a Palestinian woman is not less than her Palestinian brother, I have decided to be the second martyrdom-seeking woman and continue the path which martyr Wafā Idrees has established, and in the way of God, for taking the revenge of our martyred brothers and the trampled dignity of our religion, the mosques and the Al-Aqsā Mosque and the houses of God which have been occupied and turned into places for insulting and humiliating our religion and our Prophets and where the forbidden are committed, I offer my worthless life.

Our lives and bodies are the only things we have and we will offer them in the way of God so that we would be the bombs which will burn the Zionists and void their assumption of being the chosen people of God. The Muslim Palestinian woman, in the past and in the present, has been and is present in the frontline of the Jihad against the tyrant; therefore I call on all of my sisters to follow the path of martyrdom. Because this valley of martyrdom is the valley of all the free ones and the noble and gentle people; so whoever is after safeguarding her honor and dignity, I invite her to step in this path so that the criminal Zionists would know that our honor and dignity are nothing compared to our Jihad and resistance. So that the coward Sharon would know that every Palestinian woman would give birth to an army of martyrdom-seekers, even though he may try to settle the fear of death in the hearts of all the mothers. So that he would know that the role of woman is not limited to crying and holding the funeral of her husband, father and brother but each one of us will be a bomb at every spot to destroy the notion of Israel's security. In the end, I want all the Muslims and freedom-seekers and lovers of freedom and martyrdom to stand firm in this precious path, the path of martyrdom and freedom.

Your Martyr daughter: Dāreen Muhammad Abu-Aisheh

Martyr Ayat Muhammad Al Akhras

Date of Martyrdom: March 29, 2002

Cheers and applauses had combined with crying and tears; because it is her wedding after a few days but she is not wearing the white bridal dress. Today, she is going to see the groom who has waited for her for a year and a half. She dresses up in white dress, military dress and the Palestinian *Chafieh*[27] and with her pure blood rinses them to become the bride of Palestine to bring happiness and joy to all the mothers of the martyrs and injured.

In July 2002, Ayat Muhammad al-Akhras was supposed to get married, like any other girl; but she only wanted to go to the heavenly wedding with an outfit soaked in blood. In a heroic and successful operation in a region guarded with high security by the Zionist regime, she injured and killed dozens of Zionist invaders to glorify the Palestinian nation.

---

[27]A piece of white cloth worn over neck with special design related to Palestinian struggle.

She was supposed to have her wedding ceremony in a small house in Dheisheh[28] refugee camp. While some were expecting wailing and mourning in a wedding which they thought had been spoiled, suddenly the sound of applause came from the house. The mother of the martyr, who was welcoming the women who were congratulating her, was proudly describing her last moments with her daughter, "Ayat was up very early that morning although she had not slept at all the night before. After doing the morning prayers, she started to recite the Holy Qur'an. She wore her school uniform to go to school. I told her that today is Friday and the schools are closed. She answered, "Today is the most important day of my life." I prayed for her and asked God to help her and let her go.

Before leaving, she turned around and told me, "Mother, this (prayer) is what I want from you." And then she quickly left the house and went to school with her sister, Samah."

A tear ran down the cheek of the mother, "Around ten o'clock Samah returned home but Ayat was not with her. My heart started beating hard and I was scared. The situation was not secure and the camp could be under attack any moment. I asked where is Ayat? Where has she gone? Was it possible that she made her wish of carrying out a martyrdom-seeking operation come true? But how? And her suitor? Her wedding clothes? ... There was no end to my questions. My heart was testifying that Ayat is martyred; but I did not want to accept it. At this time, the radio announced that a young girl has carried out a martyrdom-seeking operation in the Kiryat Hayovel neighborhood of southern Jerusalem.

---

[28]Dheisheh Refugee Camp is located just south of Bethlehem in the West Bank. The Camp has a population of over 12,000.

Her mother couldn't restrain her tears, "I was sure that Ayat is gone forever, to become the bride of Palestine and take revenge of the martyrs."

Martyr Ayat al-Akhras, born on the 20th of February 1985, was a student of the third year of middle school when she was martyred. She was the fourth child of a mother and a father who had three sons and eight daughters. She had been rewarded with the best student award in the first half of 2002. Even on the last day of her life, she went to school to learn, with the help of her friends, the lessons in which she was behind and taught her classmates the importance of knowledge.

Hifa, her classmate, says, "Ayat was a serious student who was always striving to get the highest grades and she used to tell us how important it is to study nowadays... In her last week, she was collecting the pictures of all the martyrs of Intifādā, and her desk was full of verses and sayings regarding the nobleness of martyrdom and martyrs. I did not think that she wanted to go and welcome martyrdom."

With the beginning of Al-Aqsā Intifādā, Ayat tried to collect the names and photos of the martyrs, especially the ones who were martyrdom-seekers; but she thought that her wish can never be granted because she was a girl. Until Wafā Idris, a Palestinian woman, succeeded in carrying out the first martyrdom-seeking operation; this martyrdom-seeking operation gave her the motivation to pass all the obstacles and join military activity and register in the Al-Aqsā Martyrs' Brigades. Before this, she had not been a member of any organization and hadn't even participated in any of the school's activities.

Once she said of her love for martyrdom, "Now that we are surrounded by death, what is the benefit of life? We will welcome death before it comes after us and before we die, we will take the revenge." She usually tried to hide her true love for martyrdom from people.

Her sister Samah, who was her closest friend and confidant, knew that Ayat wants to carry out a martyrdom-seeking operation and when she heard about her martyrdom, she became unconscious. Afterwards, with a crying voice, she described her farewell with Ayat, "In her shining face, I saw a joy that I had not seen before. She gave me a few chocolates and with a very kind voice, said, "Pray and ask for my success." Before I could ask her the reason, she said, "Today you will receive the best news. Today is the sweetest day of my life and I have been waiting for it for a long time. Do you want me to send your salutations to anybody?" I jokingly told her to give my Salam (peace) to martyrs Mahmoud and Somayeh Saed, our neighbors who were martyred when their house was bombed with rockets. She said goodbye with all her sympathy and went for her class. I could not believe that she had such intention."

Samah stopped for a while to wipe her tears and continued, "I felt that she had an unusual look in her eyes, as if she was saying farewell to her surroundings, but I did not want to believe that! She is not capable of a martyrdom-seeking act. Who will supply her with the explosives? She is not even a member of students' association." All of a sudden, Samah's tone changed, "May she be blessed with martyrdom! She deserved it because she had the courage. I promise her that I will follow her and walk on the path of martyrdom, we are all ready to become martyrs."

Shadi Aberleban, her fiancé, was reflecting on their common wish for a son, who they would name "A'di". He was thinking of how to raise him to make him a hero who will liberate Quds from the hands of the invaders. He had been waiting to marry for more than a year; but suddenly he heard the news of the martyrdom of his dream lady in a martyrdom-seeking operation.

When asked about his fiancée, he says, "We had planned to complete our happiness after the high school examinations that year; but God, the Exalted, had written another destiny for us and I hope we will meet in paradise. That is what she has written in her last letter."

Shadi is silent for a while and looks at the picture of Ayat, "… I loved her more than I loved myself. I found her very strong, decisive, clever, and filled with love for her country and a devoted mother who wanted her kids to have a secured future. That is why the Zionist crimes disturbed her. Every time she thought about future and her dreams, the wish of being martyred always overcame. She used to talk about our union in paradise blessed by martyrdom-seeking operation and we used to promise each other for this."

Shadi, smiling, says, "In our last meeting, she kept insisting that I would stay near her; and each time I wanted to separate, she would ask me to stay, as if she was saying farewell with her kind and loving look."

Despite the sorrow that has befallen him, Shadi's voice changes all of a sudden and words which are as strong as iron and as hard as an erupting volcano full of love for his country, are what he says, "I wished that I was with her in this heroic action and that we would be martyred together.

May her martyrdom be blessed! I wish that God will soon join us together."

The Bride of Palestine, Ayat al-Akhras, will be an ideal for all the young Palestinian girls who wish for a free and secure homeland.

Martyr Andaleeb Khalil Taqatiqah

Date of Martyrdom: April 12, 2002

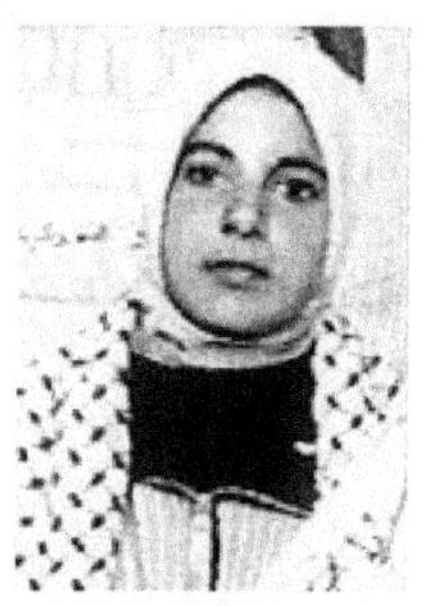

"Some people will come to seek my hand in marriage and I will welcome them." These were among the last words which were spoken by Martyr Andaleeb Taqatiqah[29] to her mother before leaving her house for the martyrdom-seeking operation.

On the 12th of April 2002, Andaleeb, in a state of haste towards her goal, left her house. The world surrounding her was burning and its homeless pigeons were flying and streams of blood were flowing on the streets. The houses of people were being demolished on their heads and the Zionist army was turning all the cities, villages and camps of the West Bank which were in the way of the Wall, into ruins. The tanks, bulldozers and aircrafts of the Zionist regime were barbarously destroying the camp of Jenin, irrespective of any human law and without any condemnation, or even attention, by any country of the region or the international community.

---

[29]Or Tagatga

Seeing the crimes and bloodshed by the occupiers, which was mixing the soil of the land of Palestine with the blood of its offspring, did not weaken her strong determination and there was no place for fear and hesitation in her heart. God had blessed her with a heart which was beating for her love for her nation and homeland and had granted her a firm ambition in which there were no signs of any doubts. She was not like other girls of her age who were always looking for the latest model of clothing and jewelry and were solely concerned with their own personal problems. She was never unmindful of her nation and homeland and their difficulties and the crimes of its occupiers.

Andaleeb was a model of simplicity and truly unique. She was like a roaring ocean filled with sorrow and grief over her nation's miseries. She was more civilized and free than those who claim to be civilized and educated and visualize liberty as an abandonment of morality and religion.

Andaleeb had reached the age of getting married and had beautiful thoughts and wishes. With this condition, 20-year old Andaleeb put away her desires to enter a new period and welcome a new life with hardships and troubles in which her wishes and feelings would be fulfilled in the best form.

Andaleeb Taqatiqah, a Palestinian girl, was born in the village of Bayt Fajjar[30], located in Bethlehem (Bayt Laham). She spent her elementary school and the beginning of middle school years over there; but due to her family's financial problems, she had to leave school in 7th grade. She started working to help her family in solving financial problems. She had eight sisters and brothers. Her oldest brother had a chronic spinal

---

[30]Bayt Fajjar is a Palestinian village, located 10 km to the southwest of the city of Bethlehem, in the southern part of West Bank. It is famous for its agriculture and industry.

column disease and one of her sisters was suffering from a heart disease. Two years before her martyrdom, Andaleeb started working in a weaving factory in Bethlehem and was working there till her martyrdom.

The true personality of this martyr is described by one of her sisters, who had a closer relationship with her, as, "Andaleeb had a strong personality and everyone respected her. She had an intimate relationship with the relatives and neighbors." She furthers says, "I believe that what influenced my sister's personality the most was the martyrdom of the infant named Iman Hajor[31]. I used to see strong signs of motivation in her, since she had started to collect different news on the genocide[32] committed in the Jenin[33] refugee camp, and while the world, especially the West, was busy enjoying its materialistic life, Andaleeb, despite the laziness and ignorance of the Arabs, was determined to stand up to assist the Palestinians and, as written in her will, to take revenge of the Zionist atrocities."

Therefore, it was not surprising that Andaleeb marched towards her set aim so that she would, with her pure blood, quench the thirst of the Holy soil of the land of Palestine, and with her blood pay the price of struggle, courage, sacrifice, dignity and honor and her blood would become the symbol of freedom and victory.

---

[31]Iman Hajor was a 4 month old Palestinian baby girl martyred by Israeli tank shelling of Khan Younis refugee camp in the Gaza on 7th May, 2001. At that time Iman Hajor was the youngest Palestinian martyr after Intifādā began.

[32]An example is that between September 2000 and May 2004, Zionist troops killed over 500 Palestinian children.

[33]Between April 3-11, 2002, Zionists troops entered Jenin refugee camp and massacred thousands of Palestinians and demolished their homes. In order to cover up their heinous crimes, the Zionist troops removed all the signs of destruction and use of unconventional weapons and no one, including UN inspection team was allowed to enter the camp for several days.

Friday, 12th of April, was the promised day and the western Quds was the location where the humiliation of the Zionists was destined, so that their arrogant walls would break down and it would be clear for everyone that the security measures taken by the Zionists are useless and defeated in front of the Palestinians' martyrdom-seeking operations.

In the western Quds, a very important event took place which afterwards cast a shadow upon everyone's thoughts. That day, Andaleeb blew up her pure body among a group of Zionists in Mahna Yahuda bazaar[34] to fulfill her duty towards God and, through her martyrdom, be a final warning for those who are indifferent and seeking worldly pleasures and those who have bought disgrace and humiliation for themselves. The explosion left 4 Zionists dead and 104 injured.

Abir, Andaleeb's sister, recalls the days before her sister's martyrdom by saying, "I gave birth to a baby who was hospitalized in the ward where immature newborns were taken care of. Suddenly, Andaleeb started insisting that we should take this child home with us. We told her that the baby would be discharged on Saturday (two days later and after her martyrdom-seeking operation). She replied that Saturday is late. We did not know what she was talking about and that she was going to carry out a martyrdom-seeking operation on Friday. Andaleeb and my mother went to get the baby, despite the presence of checkpoints and obstacles in the way. On the way home, Andaleeb had said to my mother, "Let's bother Abir and tell her that the Israeli army shot the baby!" When they reached the city, Andaleeb tried a lot to fool me but all this has become an unforgettable memory."

---

[34]Mahna Yahuda bazaar is an outdoor market in Jerusalem.

Abir further says, "This whole story happened on Thursday, which is one day before her martyrdom. Andaleeb insisted to carry the baby in her arms on the way from Al-Hanin to our home." Abir says, "Andaleeb, before her martyrdom, had told me, "Why don't you change the name of your baby and name her Andaleeb?" I told her that the name Iman is more beautiful. Andaleeb told me, "No, but Andaleeb is more beautiful.""

Abir did not know that Andaleeb was saying farewell to her and her family. She has changed the name of her baby to Andaleeb so that she would be Andaleeb's mother and now, after the arrest of her husband (which took place soon after Andaleeb's martyrdom) and his sentence to 5 years in prison on the charge of resistance against the occupiers, she is playing the role of both a mother and a father.

Andaleeb's family was surprised to learn that their martyred daughter had left a present for her sister. They found out that Andaleeb had left a little gift for the newborn baby in her cupboard. The gift was a little dress for the baby, Ayat-al-Kursi, a pair of pants for her sister and a card congratulating her sister and wishing for the newborn a life in a free homeland.

Abir, like the others, is talking as if her sister is present or has gone for some work and will return soon. She also says, "A few days before her martyrdom, Andaleeb asked me to make her some traditional sweets. I did what she had asked. Some of the raw materials of those sweets are still left and I have kept them as a memory."

Other friends and relatives of Andaleeb, like Abir, have kept, as a memory, their dear traveler – Andaleeb's - belongings such as her glasses, shirt, photos, ring… . Ahmad, Andaleeb's brother, talks about her sister's last hours, "Andaleeb woke up at 6:30 a.m. on Friday, the 12th of April 2002, and performed her morning prayers. The other members of the family were sleeping after staying up late the previous night, a long night among the nights of April in which Ariel Sharon had carried out the most widespread operation against the Palestinian nation which, in the media, became known as military incursion. Our village was besieged like the other villages and cities. In these conditions, Andaleeb woke up and prepared tea and offered it to me while I was still in my bed." Ahmad describes those memorable moments as if everything is normal. He says, "Andaleeb brought me my tea and went to the yard of the house to drink hers and afterwards make tea for her mother and tell her that today some people will come to our house for seeking my hand in marriage and ask her mother to give them a warm welcome. When her mother asks her about those people, she assures her mother by saying that she knows them and when they will come, she will be very happy because they will fulfill her wish. After a few minutes, Andaleeb casts a glance of farewell on her family and tells them that she intends to go to the garden for meditation."

Andaleeb went to a place where she wished to go and was her destiny. She, as her brother said, left the house in the morning. Ahmad, in relation to this, says, "I felt her absence. Noon came to pass… and then afternoon but she did not return. We thought that she had gone to visit one of her sisters in the village or to the house of one of the neighbors or relatives. The day was ending and she had not come back but we were not worried, even when we heard that there was a martyrdom-seeking operation in the Western Quds. It did not occur to any one of us that Andaleeb, who did not show any special interest in politics, could be the hero of this martyrdom-seeking operation, the operation which was a blow to Sharon who besieges our villages, cities and camps and commits genocides in our nation. The sun set, the midnight was approaching, and at this point we were sure that she has disappeared for some unusual reason. It was midnight when the Zionist army attacked our house and arrested some of the family members. They showed us Andaleeb's picture with her hair combed softly which was lying on the ground. We were then sure that Andaleeb, our dauntless sister who had left the home in the morning and we were worried about her, is the one who has taken the revenge of the streams of blood flowing on our homeland from the enemy."

Although the Al-Aqsā Martyrs' Brigades claimed the responsibility of the operation, Andaleeb's family insists that Andaleeb has not had any political affiliations. Her brother – Muhammad – stresses that her sister never talked about politics or any Palestinian resistance organization; but she was annoyed and fed up with the occupation and the atrocities committed by the occupiers. He points towards the fact that her sister has spent most of the hours of the nights before her martyrdom with her family and has been busy talking to them with a smile on her face; without any indication of the fact that she will soon be leaving them or that the next day she will leave the house for the martyrdom-seeking operation.

It is interesting for the whole world to know that Sunday, 14th of April 2002 (two days after her martyrdom), had been Andaleeb's birthday. This is the day which, nowadays, girls and women like to spend with partying and every year as this day approaches a lot of money is spent and the necessary items are prepared. But Andaleeb, unlike others, did not wait for her birthday party; because she had decided to celebrate it in a different place and in another form. She extinguished the fire of revenge from the occupiers which was burning in her heart on the roads of Western Quds. She, instead of blowing the candles of her 20th birthday in her father's house, lighted a million candles for the whole world and her mother was with her in this act of sacrifice. The whole of Friday, 12th of April 2002, her mother was waiting for her daughter's suitors but this wait was useless since the suitor of martyrdom had taken Andaleeb with it. That day some other people came to her house. They were not the suitors or the messengers of peace and friendship, but tens of Zionist soldiers who had their hearts filled with hate and enmity. They demolished her house around midnight and left.

It was Andaleeb and her sincerity, morality, youth, sacrifice and the depth of the love for homeland. Her union with these noble and everlasting thoughts and ideas has rendered her eternal in the age where most of the girls and women are not even aware of these values.

Martyr Heba Azem Draghema

Date of Martyrdom: May 19, 2003

She is like any other freedom lover. Those that are looking for their lost glory and the lost dignity of their homeland and in this path struggle without any complains until the Exalted God blesses them with the dawn of freedom and liberty. Those who chose to tolerate pain and grief and believe in the Divine promise of the victory of His faithful believers. She is Heba Draghema. Our speech is about Heba and all the other martyrdom-seekers who are the pride of this land. Although all the martyrdom-seekers have similar qualities, each one of them possesses a characteristic trait that makes them distinct from the others. Heba perceived a real martyrdom as the one which would guide her from this materialistic world towards the light of the hereafter and a union with her Lord and eternal peace.

Heba, who was only 19 years old on the occasion of her martyrdom, was born in the village of Toubas[35], located in Jenin. She was the youngest in the family. She had 3 sisters and 4 brothers. She finished her schooling in Toubas and entered one of the branches of al-Quds Open University in

---

[35]Toubas is located 20 km southeast of Jenin.

Jenin for continuing her education in the field of English language.

Before the end of high school and joining the university, an event occurred which was a turning point in Heba's life and placed her under a great influence; her brother Bakr decided to carry out a martyrdom-seeking operation in Israel; but, even after taking all the precautions, was arrested and ended up in a Zionist prison.

This action of her brother influenced the very depths of Heba's soul and opened her eyes to many realities and increased her awareness towards the struggle against the Zionists, the conspiracy against the Palestinian values and the dangers which were threatening her country's existence. This incident caused a great change in the course of Heba's life and her desires.

With the beginning of university life, Heba always had in her mind the fruit of the changes that had occurred in her life and an oath which she had sworn to be faithful to and fulfill it when given the opportunity.

This aim, like a luminous flame, stayed in her thoughts and wisdom until the action of the earliest female martyrdom-seekers drew her towards itself, martyrdom-seekers like Wafā Idrees, Dāreen Abu-Aisheh, Ayat al-Akhras and Andaleeb Taqatiqah. The love for carrying out a martyrdom-seeking operation overcame Heba's existence. But Heba faced many difficulties while she was investigating how to fulfill her desire for martyrdom because the Zionist army had began an extensive operation against the resistance groups in all the cities, villages and camps in the West Bank and as a result of this, many of the members of the resistance groups were either arrested or martyred and like this, the resistance lost many of its valuable forces.

Heba did not lose any hope in this situation and stayed faithful to her noble aim, until, after a passage of a few months and with the grace of God, the resistance groups were able to renovate themselves and to regain their lost forces to restart their military activities against the occupiers. Heba also saw that it was the right time to investigate the aim for which she wanted to sacrifice herself.

Finally, after a long period of endless efforts and contact with the resistance groups of Palestine, she was blessed with an opportunity to meet her Lord, and which she was awaiting very impatiently.

On Monday, 19th of May 2003, Heba for the last time saw her family and neighbors and adorned herself with a powerful explosive belt and proceeded towards her operation target. The target site was located in the city of 'Afouleh[36] in the lands which were occupied in 1948. Heba decided to enter the Hakim shopping mall through its eastern door and blow herself up among the Zionists but she couldn't. Therefore, she blew herself up near the entrance door. In this heroic operation, at least 3 were killed and 70 were injured.

Of course the damage could have been greater than this; but before the explosion, the guard of the mall became suspicious of her and did not permit Heba to enter the mall. Thus, she was forced to blow herself up in the vicinity of the mall's entrance.

The news of this operation quickly spread everywhere and people became aware of the identity of the one who had

---

[36]Located in the east of Jerusalem.

carried it out. Her family members, after hearing this news, did not believe that their daughter had carried out such an operation because they thought that she was at the university, attending her classes.

Misa al-Toubassi, Heba's neighbor, says, "When Heba's father heard from different people that his daughter has carried out a martyrdom-seeking operation, he immediately went to his house but did not find Heba over there. Then, he went to the houses of three of Heba's sisters who are married but saw that Heba is not there as well. They said that the last time they saw Heba was when she was going to the university around 1 p.m. At that moment, he realized the truth of what the people of the village were saying."

Misa further said, "When the news spread, a feeling of wonder and surprise filled the village. None of the village inhabitants were able to believe that Heba, who was known to everyone as a very quiet girl, would carry out a martyrdom-seeking act."

News about the group responsible for this operation was unusual. Both the Al-Aqsā Martyrs Brigades and the Quds Battalion[37] separately claimed the responsibility of this operation.

According to the sources close to the martyr's family, Heba did not have any connections with any organizations nor did she have any political affiliations. But some sources say that she was one of the active members of the Students' Islamic Association of the Jihad-e-Islami Movement in the branch of al-Quds Open University in Jenin.

---

[37]Al-Quds Battalion is a military wing of Islamic Jihad (*Jihad-e-Islami*) Movement.

In addition, many of the supporters of the Jihad-e-Islami Movement of Palestine distributed pictures of Heba adorned with a headband with *"La ilā hā illā Allah"* written on it and a flag of the Jihad-e-Islami Movement in the background.

In any case, whether the Al-Aqsā Martyrs' Brigades or the Quds Battalion were behind this operation, it doesn't make any difference because it was Heba who became the best model of sacrifice and with her pure blood and eternal martyrdom laid out a firm foundation for achieving dignity and honor.

Martyr Hanādi Tissir Jarādāt

Date of Martyrdom: October 4, 2003

Unlike other lawyers, she did not want to defend her rights in a courtroom where justice and truth had no place; but she took hold of a different way to make everybody listen her voice and understand what she had in her mind.

Martyr Hanādi Jarādāt was a lawyer who carried out a martyrdom-seeking operation on the 4th of October 2003 in Maxim restaurant in Haifa (located in the lands occupied in 1947) and this way, she took the revenge of the blood of innocent martyrs and the oppressed people of Palestine who were targeted by the Zionist terrorists.

Hanādi was an example of a Muslim, a believing and religious girl who was aware of the right given by the God, the Creator to the religion and her nation and sacrificed her life for this right.

She cast aside the materialistic pleasures of life and this world and, with her heart and soul, went towards the Lord to achieve His satisfaction and paradise. She, filled with the fear of God's anger, was always reading the Holy Qur'an and praying and these deeds were taking her closer to God and they brought confidence and peace to her.

She was not afraid of death, never got tired of difficulties, and never gave up because she was daily witnessing how the bodies of the martyrs were falling on the ground and the holy land of Prophets was being colored with their blood.

Four years had passed since Sharon had dishonored the Al-Aqsā Mosque with his presence and the Intifādā had begun, but her hatred and grudge for the Zionists had not lessened at all. She had concluded that she would not have any future with her law degree since the human rights are trampled upon openly in this world and nobody dares to speak up. She was not interested in doing the practical exercises in law and wanted to practice it in reality, which means in the great court which had witnessed the martyrdom of innocent children, disrespect to the women and the martyrdom of Muhammad al-Durāh in the arms of his father.

Hanādi Jarādāt was born on the 22nd of September 1975 in Hay al-Sharqi[38] in Jenin. Her family comprised eight daughters, two sons and parents. She was 29 years old when she was martyred.

She completed her middle and high school in Al-Zahrā school and then went to Jordan and got admission in the Jarash University. She wanted to study law so that she could raise her voice against the occupiers and defend the rights of the prisoners who were struggling against the occupiers. She graduated in 1999 and received a Bachelor's degree in this field. In 2001, she joined special courses for practicing law to defend the rights of her oppressed nation. She was practicing

---

[38]The East Quarter

her job until the last day of her everlasting life and wanted to open an office for herself as an independent lawyer.

The criminal Zionists attacked her house on the 14th of June 2003 and martyred her brother, Fādi, and her cousin, Sāleh, in front of her eyes. Since then, Hanādi was living for taking the revenge of the blood of those two. This crime affected her personality and life and made her ready to seek revenge and no one could prevent her.

Fādieh, Hanādi's sister, describes her sister's behavior before the martyrdom, "Since my brother's martyrdom, Hanādi's attitude changed completely. She liked to be alone and isolated. She would listen to religious cassettes, read Qur'an and would not laugh like she used to before."

Fādieh added, "The martyrdom of Fādi motivated Hanādi to carry out the martyrdom-seeking operation. But the most important of all, which lighted the fire of grudge and hatred inside her chest, was what was happening in Palestine every day and affected everyone, like massacres, killing, demolishing of the houses and detaining. She was not just motivated by the martyrdom of Fādi and Sāleh. The scenes shown on the television are good enough to create a bomb out of every Palestinian."

Fādieh describes her sister, "My sister was known for her courage among the girls of her age. She had a strong character and nobody could change her mind. She was a very social person and loved everyone and everybody loved her too. If she would see a poor person, she would ask us to feed him, telling us that God will give us a great reward."

Fādieh continued, "She was against the music that made her forget God and she was more devoted to religion after she graduated in law from the university in Jordan. She was closer to God and had completely stopped listening to *harām* (forbidden) music and songs."

She was looking in the Quds Battalion, the military branch of Islamic Jihad, to fulfill her wish against the Zionists. And then she waited to perform what she wanted to so that she could extinguish the fire of hatred and revenge inside her.

Finally the promised day arrived and Hanādi, with a heart of full of joy, was ready to meet her Lord. Since two weeks before the operation, she had started to fast every day and she prayed, read the Holy Qur'an and stayed up during the nights more than before.

In the night before her martyrdom, she was deeply connected to God and by reading the verses of victory, asked God to help her and give her the courage for keeping her promise. She was continuously reciting the Holy Qur'an. That night, her father insisted that she should get some sleep but she refused and said that she has to read the last part of the Qur'an. In her last night, she did not sleep at all. She was praying all night and reading the Qur'an and asking God to help her in the martyrdom-seeking operation and make her wish come true.

On the morning of Saturday, 4th of October 2003, she left the house around 7:30 and did not say goodbye to anybody since she did not want to have anybody's attention. Everyone thought that she was going to her office. She was fasting that day. She went to Haifa, located in the lands occupied in 1948, to the Maxim restaurant[39] so that she could witness the awaited bloody day.

---

[39]The Maxim restaurant is a famous beachfront restaurant located near the south entry to Haifa city. Famous Zionist personalities dine at this restaurant.

She calmly entered the restaurant and ordered food. She had her food without showing any signs of anxiety and without getting excited and disturbed. She paid her bill and suddenly showed the Zionists her anger towards them and pulled the trigger of the explosive belt which she had around herself. In this martyrdom-seeking operation, twenty two Zionists were killed and dozens were injured.

The police and other forces of the Zionist regime were shocked when they found out that she had had her last meal, had paid the bill calmly, and then carried out the operation. The police and the National Security (Shabak) did not believe that she had done this but they had to when they found the proof in the cash register because before she had carried out the operation to meet her Lord, she had paid 90 Shekels (20 Dollars).

In their simple and small house, after hearing the news, her family was grateful to God. Her father was suffering from a liver disease and said, "I do not welcome any condolences, but I do welcome the congratulations, because what my daughter did is my honor."

Her mother was proud of her too because she had taken the revenge of the blood of the Palestinian martyrs.

Hanādi is gone but her spirit is there, on the streets, in all the camps, cities, and villages of Palestine and witnessing our lives. She has left but her memory will stay in the heart of each Palestinian, Arab, and Muslim, as a model of courage and devotion forever.

The Video Testament of Martyr Hanādi Jarādāt

"In the name of God, the Compassionate, the Merciful"

With the help of God, I have decided to be the sixth martyrdom-seeking woman who blows up her body to kill the Zionists and destroy the settlers and the Zionists. We are not willing to do this just for paying back the Zionists for their crimes so that our mothers do not mourn anymore but we want to do something to make the Zionist mothers mourn their sons. So, with the help of God, I have decided to surround the Zionists with death the way they have surrounded us and do something to make their mothers mourn them. I pray to God to bless us with paradise and send them to hell.

Your martyrdom-seeking daughter
Hanādi Tissir Jarādāt
3rd October, 2003

Martyr Reem Saleh al-Riyāshi

Date of Martyrdom: January 14, 2004

The day of Wednesday, 14th of January 2004, is not considered an ordinary day in the history of Palestine and the resistance of this nation because this day is the reminiscent of a martyrdom-seeking Palestinian mother named Reem Saleh al-Riyāshi, who on the occasion of her martyrdom was only 22 years old. She is considered as the first martyrdom-seeking woman in the movement of Hamās and the Gaza Strip. Despite the fact that Reem is the 7th martyrdom-seeking Palestinian woman who carried out a martyrdom-seeking operation against the Zionists, her operation differs greatly with the other similar operations; because she was the first mother who, with her martyrdom, left alone her two children and husband. Her youngest child was only 18 months old when she was martyred. Through this operation, her name was registered in the list which contains the heroic names of Wafā Idrees, Dāreen Abu Aisheh, Ayat al-Akhras, Andaleeb Taqatiqah, Heba Dragmeh and Hanādi Jarādāt. Her character and action, which are manifested in the papers she left behind, are quite distinct than the others. Even the time and place of her martyrdom-seeking operation were different than of the ones before. She came at the beginning of the year 2004 to once again awaken the spirit of resistance. The location of her operation was one of the most secure bases of the occupiers. With her sharp blow to the Bani Zion, once again the Islamic resistance and her martyrdom-seeking displayed their power to shatter the myth of the strength of the Zionist regime.

Reem al-Riyāshi is the symbol of esteem and honor and a symbol of dignity of the Islamic nation of Palestine, who has been restless while awaiting such unique model of sacrifice and faith. She pushed aside the obstacles of fear, weakness, and inability, which are found in the way to perfection by every person.

Reem al-Riyāshi combined the power of faith, strength of belief, firmness of willpower, profundity of sacrifice and the tender motherly affection with each other. She was like a peak of a high mountain that crushed the haughtiness and pride of the Zionists in the modern era.

Reem al-Riyāshi was a mother like all the other mothers, but as much as she lived for her religion and homeland, she did not live for herself and her children. She was more devoted to her religion and country than to herself and her children. Therefore she deserved to be the most honored martyrdom-seeker and the flag-holder of the struggle and Jihad of a Muslim woman on the Palestinian soil.

Since long before her martyrdom-seeking operation, she had been taking steps in the way of martyrdom and never gave up hope until finally God bestowed upon her the blessing of martyrdom. Her martyrdom was a victory for the Jihad and the freedom movement over the Zionist terrorists.

She was a great treasure of spirituality. She, with her historical operation, calmed down the heart of her nation; but for the Zionists, she was like a fiery and eruptive volcano. She believed that faith can cause miracles and a connection with God and help from Him can lift all the obstacles from the way.

She had the belief that as long as she did not stray from the path of God, she would never lose her way and in the end, she will succeed and the victory would be hers.

She did not come up with the instinct of motherhood as an excuse to give up the duty of Jihad. She could not close her eyes to the destruction of her country, her nation and her ideals. Her motherhood wasn't in conflict with reality, truth, faith and justice and for this reason she was ready to sacrifice her life for her belief in God and her love for her Lord, without her heart being affected by religious doubts or emotional feelings. She returned what she was trusted with to its owner.

Saleh, Reem's father, was the representative of a German factory, which produced car batteries, and was fairly well off. Her family consisted of six brothers and four girls and she was the third daughter. Since her childhood, this girl, like all the Saleh family members, was religious and devoted to the teachings of Islam in all the areas of her life. During her life, she took steps in the path of obedience to God and love for His messenger, religion and believers. She started going to mosque frequently at very young age. 'Mustafa' mosque was where she found out about what was valuable and learned the essential principles and thoughts which would promise her a virtuous life, a life far from extravagance, luxury and profanations. She joined the Students' Islamic Association of Hamās during the years of university education. Islamic values, principles, and thoughts gradually developed and flourished in Reem's heart and soul and with every day that passed, her love for her religion and homeland increased until she officially joined Hamās and became one of its most active members in the area where she lived. Along with going to the mosques, she regularly read and studied religious books, used to carry out her religious duties such as fasting and *nafilah* (non-obligatory optional prayers) and held religious lessons for women in Mustafa mosque.

When she reached the age of getting married, many young men, who were fascinated by her punctuality, conduct, piety and nobility, came to seek her hand. But Reem was not like other ordinary girls to ask for worldly luxuries and with an insightful eye, she was looking at the faraway horizon and the other world. She did not accept what other girls eagerly desire and agree to and was not misled and deceived by money and wealth, family background, social class and many other qualities that were possessed by a large number of her suitors.

Reem placed a condition for her suitors, which was very startling in this modern age in which the valuable has become insignificant and the invaluable has turned significant. Her condition was that if she would marry him, then her husband should not stop her from her political and religious activities, including martyrdom-seeking operation. This condition was very hard to accept for many of the young men who wanted to marry her. But some accepted. One of them was Ziād Awād, a young man with 28 years of age, who accepted her condition and became her husband and partner in this world. They started living together in 'Hay al-Zaytoun', located in the eastern part of the city of Gaza. God blessed them with two kids; both of them were less than 3 years old in January 2004.

Unlike many young people, the family life and the love of husband and children did not change her and calm her down. With every day that passed, her love for martyrdom increased. She believed that she has lived long enough and it is time for her martyrdom. She, when in high school, had intended to carry out a martyrdom-seeking operation. In those years, she used to pray to God that He would open up the way for her martyrdom in the lands occupied in 1948; but she was not successful in acting upon her wish. She continued her try for achieving her goal and never became hopeless and desperate. She even enrolled her name as a volunteer for martyrdom-seeking operation in the Qassām Brigades headquarters, but they refused due to the conditions at that time.

Reem was hoping to see God and to do Jihad in His path, until Intifādā provided her with the means of blowing herself up among the enemies of God and humanity, since many *mujahidins* had sacrificed their lives and carried out martyrdom-seeking operations in the West-Bank to struggle.

Being married and giving birth to two kids was not an obstacle for Reem in fulfilling her wish and she constantly insisted on the Qassām Brigades for letting her carry out a martyrdom-seeking operation but they hesitated since she was a mother and a wife. Her courage and faith convinced the Qassām Brigades and they agreed to select her as the first martyrdom-seeking mother although there were many girls and women ready for the action.

To choose her was not an easy decision for Martyr Izz ad-Din al-Qassām Brigades and there were a lot of discussions and deliberations before she was allowed. Of course, there was no restriction on the participation of woman in the struggle against the Zionist enemy. And that is why she was allowed.

They contacted her and she became ready for this operation. There was no further need for any special training on how to pull the trigger or to cover up to avoid suspicions since Reem's iron willpower and love for martyrdom had a greater share in determining the success of her mission.

Before the operation, it was necessary that Reem should visit the site of the operation. She carefully watched the Erez crossing in Bayt Hanoun[40] to her residence and observed how the Zionist soldiers inspected the people daily. She also made a few suggestions regarding the operation.

With the help of God, everything was ready and everyone was waiting for the operation to be carried out so that once more the lives of the Zionists would be turned into hell.

After the operation, the Palestinian Resistance movement (Hamās) revealed some of the obstacles they had faced in allowing this operation to be carried out. Osamah Hamdān, the Hamās representative in Lebanon, gave the details, "Reem was one of the first women to volunteer for the martyrdom-seeking operation. She had given this request to the movement three years ago and she had insisted on the agreement of martyrdom-seeking act. But the military branch of the movement did not agree. It was only a few months ago that the military branch accepted women to participate in these operations. After getting permission from her husband, she also got the permission from the battalion."

Hamdān added, "From a religious point of view, Hamās did not have any problem with women carrying out martyrdom-seeking operation. This is because we believe that when an

---

[40]The town of Bayt Hanoun is located in the north of Gaza strip and Erez crossing is one of the main checkpoints occupied by Zionist soldiers. Several patients including pregnant women have died at the Israeli checkpoints.

enemy attacks the land of Muslims, Jihad is obligatory for every Muslim man or woman. But the carrying out of a martyrdom-seeking operation by a woman needed special permission from the military headquarters. So, this was discussed with the Qassām brigades and they finally approved. There were many positive consequences of these operations. All the resistance groups of Palestine (Hamās, Jihad-e-Islami and Fatah) approve of the participation of women in the martyrdom-seeking operations because resistance is our only way, regardless of who continues it."

The day of the operation was set as Wednesday, 14th of January 2004, since Wednesday is the day of women. This day was unique in the Palestinian and the Zionist history. The hearts of the Palestinians were filled with peace and tranquility when they heard the news of this operation but this news was like a great thunderbolt for the Zionist regime which left them in a shock and shook their very foundation.

Carrying out this operation was not easy but very hard and was based on careful planning and most of all, on the divine grace. The Erez crossing in Bayt Hanoun was a military fortress protected by hundreds of Zionist soldiers, ready to destroy any uprising among the people. On the morning of operation, Reem put on an explosive belt and walked straight to the target. She walked on the same path as the other women, the path which was filled with Zionist soldiers and checkpoints. Everything was fine until Reem passed under the electronic detector. The sensor detected the metal under her clothes. The soldiers wanted to take her to a special room for inspection. But there were no signs of anxiety or any other reactions from her and she started walking with them. At that very instant, she realized that the time for her holy mission has arrived and she pulled the trigger and brought devastation to the Zionists. Four Zionists were killed and ten others were injured. The myth of the passage of Erez in Bayt Hanoun being a secure place was also over. This passage, which connects the Gaza Strip to the lands which were occupied in 1948, was extremely difficult to pass and only workers with special permission were permitted to be in the area. But Reem, while carrying powerful explosives, managed to pass all the checkpoints and obstacles and by deceiving the Zionists, get into this high security fortress. She blew herself up in order to make the Zionists taste the death the way they had been making the Palestinians taste it.

While the Zionists were collecting the bodies of the dead soldiers and cleaning up the rubble after this operation, General Gadi Shamni, the commander of the Zionist soldiers in the Gaza Strip, during an interview, said, "The executioner of this operation succeeded in deceiving the soldiers in charge of the checkpoints before carrying out the operation."

The radio of the Zionist regime, reporting Shamni's statements, said, "The executioner of operation claimed to have a piece of platinum installed in her leg." According to this Zionist general, the executioner of this operation used the ingredients available to the Palestinians in the Gaza Strip to carry out this operation.

Two days later, a young man was standing in front of the freezer which kept dead bodies in Dar-Ashafa hospital in the Gaza city. He was Ziād Awād, Reem's husband. One of the girls of the family was holding 'Zahi' and was crying and another woman was holding 'Muhammad', the baby infant, and she was crying as well. Everyone was crying. Her husband and relatives were preparing the coffin for the body of Reem, which was in pieces and covered with a green flag with the slogan of *"La ilā hā illā Allah"* (There is no deity except Allah).

Ziād, before saying anything, was very proud of his wife. He said, "Reem was a model of a virtuous, pious and devoted wife. The crimes of the Zionists were her motivation for carrying out this heroic martyrdom-seeking operation. She left her two children to join the caravan of the Palestinian martyrs. She was a loyal wife and the best partner and her memory will live in the hearts of all the Palestinians who are seeking freedom. My wife, Umme Muhammad, was a mother with great spiritual ideas and thoughts and this is how she wanted to meet her Creator."

Ziād Awād, who is a lifeguard on the coast of the Gaza Sea, added, "It was rare to see my wife, Reem, crying. But when she would see the scenes of the crimes of the invaders, their terrorist acts, the blessed body of martyrs, the demolished houses in Rafah, Jenin, Shojaiyeh, Hay al-Zaytoun, Jabālia and Al-Aqsā Mosque, she would cry and would feel sorry for the condition of the Al-Aqsā Mosque. She grew up in a religious house full of love and faith. That is why she was blessed with martyrdom and became our pride. She deserved martyrdom. What my wife did is an action of honor and pride for us and the Islamic nation and all the Arab and Islamic countries. This is the blessing of God, which he has bestowed upon us for her holy action. What Reem did is the Jihad which is an obligation on every Palestinian man and woman."

Ziad said, "Reem participated in all kinds of Jihad she could, no matter how insignificant, against the Zionists before her martyrdom. She was devoted to take food to all combatants, especially those who were on duty for information, identification and safety in the area. Even on the day before her martyrdom, she distributed cake and tea among the *mujahidins*."

He said about his marriage with Reem, "Her attitude and behavior was very simple and based on morality and our traditions in Gaza. But she had placed some conditions for her suitors. One of them was that her husband should not prevent her from fasting, staying up all night for praying and Jihad. And let her have her Islamic hijab. All her efforts and activities were related to the worship of God. Reem learned how to use weapons in the Hamās movement. Her insistence on learning this was one of the signs of her intense love for martyrdom. Because they had stopped her from Jihad activities, she repeatedly used to say that I wish I was a man so that I could struggle in the path of God. From this point of view, she liked weapons and learning to shoot.

Since middle school, she loved Jihad and martyrdom in the way of God. And so, she always went to the houses of martyrs and *mujahidins* and asked the leaders of the movement to let her take part in a martyrdom-seeking operation.

Although her wish was refused each time but she kept insisting and finally God accepted her wish. The day they told her that she has been chosen for the operation was the best day of her life."

Awād said about the selection of Reem for the martyrdom-seeking operation, "The commander of The Qassām Brigades chose Reem when he noticed that she is insisting too much in this field and if she is not helped, she would do it on her own. She was extremely happy from the moment they told her that she is on her way for the action. Reem prayed and fasted more than before. Reem fasted on her last days and even on the day of the operation so that she could go to her God while fasting and be the best model of honesty and sincerity towards God and sacrifice herself for the sake of her religion and beliefs and for loyalty to her nation and its sacraments. On the day of the operation, unusual boldness and strength was observable in her. When they brought her a 10-kg explosive belt, she was asking for a heavier one so that she could send more Zionists to hell."

Ziad Awād talked about Reem's social relations and her last moments with her children, "She had a very natural relation with everybody and was a caring mother. On her last day she had an unimaginably high spirit. She kissed her kids and left, as if she is going on a minor trip. She told me that her children should be brought up with Islamic disciplines and should memorize Qur'an. It was her will that her jewelry, some gold she had and $1000 should be spent for the construction of a mosque so that it would be a *sadaqaye jariya*[41] for her and her husband and another 1400 dinars should be given to a person to attend Haj on her behalf. She also left around 30,000 Jordanian dinars as an inheritance for her family from which, as she said, 5000 dinars would be spent as a charity on her late father's behalf and the rest for the mosque as a charity on her behalf. In her last moments she read some verses of Qur'an and asked me to distribute sweets among people after her martyrdom. In her last moment, she asked forgiveness from me. I said, "Why are you asking this?" She answered, "I want you to forgive me." I said, "It is God who should forgive and will forgive.""

Ziād pointed to his children and said, "I will tell my daughter Zahi and my son Muhammad that your mother carried out a martyrdom-seeking operation. I am thankful to God for giving your mother the opportunity to kill four and injure ten

---

[41] An Islamic term which means that the reward of a charity or good act done by a person continues as long as society or people benefit from it, even after his/her death. For example construction of a library, school, etc

Zionists. I will tell them to not to worry. God, the Exalted, will take care of you and will give you peace and patience. I pray to God to make my children happy in the future and, with His grace, they would memorize Qur'an."

Ziād denied the news published by the Zionist media about the disputes between him and his wife, "This is an utter untruth. I thank God that we had a wonderful life together and she always used to tell me that she passed her sweetest times with me."

Reem's family said that although they were not aware of her intention but they were very proud of what she did.

Iman Riyashi, her brother, said, "What my sister did is a great honor for the Gaza Strip and the Palestinian nation. Her love for Islam and Palestine was her motivation for this martyrdom-seeking operation against the Zionist occupiers. We were not aware of her holy intention and never even noticed anything unusual in her the last time we saw her and she had not changed at all."

Saif, another one of Reem's brothers, said, "I did not even feel for a moment that inside my sister's peaceful heart, there is anger and rage hidden or that she would leave her kids. But when I see her video testament will and hear what she said, I feel proud and I thank God."

All the people of the region were also proud of Reem and her Jihad against the Zionist occupiers. Muhammad Arabi, 21 years old, said, "In the region of Tal al-Hawa[42] the atmosphere is such as if it is the wedding of the first martyrdom-seeking mother of the Gaza Strip."

---

[42]Tal al-Hawa is a neighborhood in the south of Gaza City.

After this operation, many asked themselves, "Where was Reem's motherly love when she left her kids to blow herself up in a martyrdom-seeking operation in the passage of Bayt Hanoun in the north of the Gaza Strip? Did she lose this feeling? Or did another feeling take its place?"

It is clear that a different feeling overcame this motherly love. It is the feeling which is known by the psychologists as the strongest one and it is faith which comes into existence in the hearts of Muslims and which makes them sacrifice their most precious belongings to get rid of oppression, to free their homeland and to reach paradise.

Analysts and experts point towards the fact that the martyrdom-seeking operation of Reem had been a difficult one due to its site, the presence of numerous security obstacles and the spiritual qualities that these operations require such as courage, strength and iron willpower. These qualities were what made her calmly walk among the Zionist soldiers and pull the trigger of the explosives and shred the Zionists into pieces.

At the moment of explosion, the atmosphere of the passage of Bayt Hanoun filled with cries, screams and pieces of stones and glass. Blood covered the walls and the ground and the smell of death spread everywhere.

It is without a doubt that the motherly love is the strongest feeling but what Reem did was the zenith of all the human feelings. People usually think of motherly love as a concern for children, especially the younger ones. Reem, with her martyrdom and leaving two kids, showed that she doesn't only have a strong feeling for her kids but for all the children of her oppressed nation. This feeling matured inside her because of her belief and faith in Islam. Her children are the children of all the mothers of Islam.

Reem al-Riyāshi embraced martyrdom in an era in which most of the women are not even ready to give up their cell phones for one day let alone their children, husbands and families. Reem was and will be, forever, the epitome of sacrifice in the way of religion and sacraments.

The Last Will of Reem al-Riyāshi for the Women and Children of the Nation

My dear sisters and children of the oppressed Arab nation! Do allow me to address you before the operation which I intend to carry out soon and I ask the All-Mighty God to accept my martyrdom and help me kill as many Zionist soldiers as possible.

You are responsible for the leadership and guidance of this nation to victory, dignity, and honor. You are the flag bearer of this nation, holding this flag among the flags of other nations living on this earth. O women of nation! Children will be born and raised by you who will bring victory and dignity to the nation and they will do that with their blessed bloods and bodies. Among the children of this nation, there will be some who will train others to throw stones and to stand up against the tanks with bare chests to free this nation from degraded leaders, base and low persons, hypocrites and the Jewish occupiers and to bring this nation back to its real position among the East and the West.

But, I advise popular leaders to stop talking, and I ask our current rulers to come down from their seats because they are not worthy of leading people.

Oh sisters! I ask God to accept me as a martyr. I hope to see Him and I want to complain to Him against those who have betrayed Quds and Palestine and its people. I will testify against all of those who, to show their obedience, bowed to their bosses in the White House and did not even help our children. I will testify against all of those who sought help from the Jews and did not accept help from their Muslim brothers. I will testify against all of those who fought with their own people but stopped the war against the enemy. I will testify against all of those who, instead of living for their nation, lived for their throne and comfort and sold their country. I will testify against those who sent away the righteous and replaced them with the sinful and corrupt. I will testify against those who brought weakness and made us afraid of the enemy.

I will testify against those who stole the money of this nation, and placed it in their and their relatives' bank accounts and left their people so that they would not have to face the misery they were facing.

I want to testify against those government-paid religious scholars, who order the fatwa[43] of obeying the ruler and forbid disobedience to them. These are devils who only say things which secure their statuses and earnings. They speak things where they should not be spoken and fall silent where they should not be silent. They, in their opinion, want to bring an end to sedition when there is none. They accuse each one of their brothers of heresy but obey and stay silent in front of the rulers and urge people to obey them as well. After my martyrdom, you will hear a lot of things. Some will say that I killed myself. Some will say that I committed suicide

---

[43] Religious order issued by highest level of authority.

and some will even say that how stupid she was to leave her children and husband and did not keep her family's respect.

But I say: I am a believer and God bestowed upon me these children and will raise them up after me.

You will find out that the real sustainer of all and everything is only God. Everything is in His hands. He does not hire anyone and no one hires Him. At the end, I remind all of you on the behalf of Palestine and the Holy Al-Aqsā Mosque, Iraq and all the Islamic countries that these are (Godly given) trust in your hands.

Was-Salam

Video Testament of Reem al-Riyāshi

I, martyrdom-seeker Reem al-Riyāshi, am a member of Martyr Izz ad-Din al-Qassām Brigades. I am doing this operation, with the co-operation of my brothers in Al-Aqsā Martyrs' Brigades, only for attaining the satisfaction of God and to take revenge from the Jews, the enemies of humanity and those who are corrupting my land, in Rafah, Nablus, Ramallah, Jenin and the rest of the cities and to wipe away some of the shame brought to this land by the wrongdoings of its conspiratorial rulers who are co-operating with the enemy.

My Heroic People!
As soon as they give us a blow, we will take our revenge and the fire of this resistance will be ablaze till it burns our Jewish enemies and firmly places the flag of Tawhid (monotheism) all over our dear homeland and on the minarets of the Al-Aqsā Mosque. I ask you to pray for my success and endurance.

And I want to ask God, the Glorious, to accept my action only for His sake and to bring misery to the Zionists and to give tranquility to the hearts of all the believers.

And He is Guardian of this matter and has all power to do it

And the last words,

All praise belongs to Allah, the Lord of all the worlds

Shaheed Izz ad-Din al-Qassām Brigades and the Al-Aqsā Martyrs' Brigades

***

In the name of Allah, the Beneficent, the Merciful

Verily, Jihad is an obligation on every Muslim. God says, *"Indeed Allah had bought from the faithful their souls and their possessions for paradise to be theirs"* [Qur'an, 9:111] and so, Jihad through offering your life is superior to Jihad through offering your belongings and all of those who are killed in Jihad are considered martyrs, no matter if they are killed in Palestine, Iraq, Bosnia or Chechnya.

Oh people! Do you want to know what the status of a martyr near God is? There are 7 kinds of rewards for martyrs: 1. All of his sins are forgiven as soon as the first drop of his blood spills. 2. He is saved from the punishment in grave. 3. He is saved from the great punishment on the Day of Judgment. 4. Hoor al ain come to marry him. 5. A crown is placed on his head which has a jewel more precious than this world and what it contains. 6. He will be allowed to intercede for seventy of his family members. 7. He sees his place in paradise.

The land of Palestine will be the land of *mujahidins* and warriors till the Day of Judgment. God says, *"Make war on them so that Allah may punish them by your hands and humiliate them, and help you against them, and heal the hearts of a faithful folk."* [Qur'an, 9:14]

I greatly longed for and awaited martyrdom. So, how fortunate and happy I would be if God accepts me as a martyr. By God, my heart is filled with different feelings and I cannot control these feelings. This thought is victorious over my reason and this awareness has entered my heart and a beautiful tranquility has embraced my existence and each one of my heartbeats is saying, "Oh God! Consider me a martyr near you!"

How much I had wished and imagined that one day my body would turn into violent thunder which would shred Bani Zion into pieces and that I would be able to reach the doors of Heaven with their skulls.

By God, even if my bones are broken and my body is cut into pieces, they will not be able to take my religion away from me and snatch down its flag from me. This is my situation.

How many times I told myself, "Oh my existence! Know that my spirit is filled with hatred towards these Jewish enemies, so create a way for me to paradise out of you."

I had started my search and struggle since I was in 10th grade. I searched constantly on a daily basis to find someone who would guide me to achieve my goal or help me or answer my questions. By God, I searched for many years but I did not get tired nor did I have a feeling of regret, not even for one moment. To find someone who would assent to my wish, which is to embrace martyrdom, was very difficult.

How patient I was and how much I wished to carry out a martyrdom-seeking operation in Israel (lands occupied in 1948) but I did not succeed. How much I waited to offer my existence to God. By God, I desired to be the first woman to carry out a martyrdom-seeking operation. But on the condition that my body would disperse in air into pieces and that they would know me for this action and remember me and… These were blessings what I had asked for from God, the gloried and the magnificent. Finally, with endless struggle and divine grace and blessing, my desire reached fulfillment in the way I had wanted.

Indeed, I have turned to God so that on the Day of Judgment I would stand beside Him and declare, "Oh my Lord! This is my body which I have offered in your way." And by the grace of God, I got to know a group of faithful believers in the 2nd year of high school and also finished my training.

Oh God! Make me a weapon one day so that the bullets fired from my body would tear apart the bodies of Bani Zion[44].

After military training and familiarity with weapons, I reached a conclusion that with the help of God, it is possible for a small group to be victorious over a large group.

Right now, it is my existence which is saying, "Until faith is in my heart and is carrying my weapon, God will provide me with the opportunity of Jihad and the destruction of enemies."

Until before the recording of this video tape, I did not think that I would be able to say anything, but now I want to say that happiness has filled my heart and I am now getting

---

[44]The followers of Zionism

ready to see my Lord and I have prepared myself to be presented in His court and I hope that He blesses me with accepting my present.

Oh God! I love your company. Please, you, too, love my company.

Even though I have two children, both of which are gifts from God and only He knows how much I love them, but I love to see God more. I entrust these children to my family and I am convinced that they will grow up under God's care.

I want you to teach my children *dhikr*[45] and obedience and to plant seeds of religion and faith in them. Make efforts so that they would memorize Qur'an and receive education in Islamic schools. I am entrusting these two (kids) to you and I will ask you about them on the Day of Judgment. Our reunion will be in paradise. Insha Allah.

I advise you to be pious. I charge you to honor and respect Palestinian fighters. When you bury me, distribute cassettes of the Qur'anic recitation and give away the money for ceremonies as charity because there are plenty of needy people. Pray for me in the great mosque of Al-Am'ari[46]. Also, I ask you to bury me, if possible, near the graves of martyrs and the righteous. My grave should be on the ground level and don't raise it. I want you to pray that God considers this act of mine solely for Himself. I thank every fighter who steps on this blessed land.

For the sake of God, just write on my grave:
"Martyr Reem Saleh al-Riyāshi"

---

[45]Remembrance of God
[46]Al-Am'ari refugee camp

Martyr Zainab Ali Abu Salem

Date of Martyrdom: September 22, 2004

On Wednesday, 6th of Sha'ban 1425, coincident with the 22nd of September 2004, after a huge explosion in 'Tel-al-Faransiya' (French Hill), in the city of Quds (Jerusalem), 35 Zionist occupiers were injured out of which 3 were killed. Few minutes later, Al-Aqsā Martyrs' Brigades the military division of the Fatah movement, by sending a proclamation to the world media, claimed the responsibility of the explosion in the area of 'Tel-al-Faransiya' and introduced the one who had carried it out, and in this way, the name of the 18 year old Palestinian Zainab Ali Isa Abu Salem was recorded in the history of the Jihad of the Islamic Ummah against the Zionist invaders as the 10th martyrdom-seeking Palestinian woman.

This brave young lady was one of inhabitants of the Askar[47] refugee camp. She was the fourth of ten children in her family, who were well off for Palestinians. They owned the

---

[47]Askar is located on the outskirts of the West Bank city of Nablus. It was established in 1950 and then extended further. It has population of over 15,000. Zionist forces frequently invade this camp.

television station where she appeared on a children's show. She lived with her aunt, Salwa Abu Salem, a 49 year old teacher and a dozen people in one house. Zainab had just graduated from high school and was planning to go to college for further education.

Martyr Zainab had the intention of getting herself inside one of buses transporting the Zionist settlers but was recognized and stopped by the Zionist police. They asked to see her identity papers and search the bag she was carrying on her back. She argued for a few seconds then detonated her bomb, killing the two Zionists at the spot.

'Tel-al-Faransiya' is a place where a large number of Zionists gather daily to get to the Zionist settlements through the buses. Following this operation, the Zionist military analysts and authorities seriously questioned the efficacy of the numerous strict security policies and checkpoints in the occupied Palestine. How could an 18 year old girl with an appearance which completely reveals her Arab origin and meanwhile having the Islamic hijab manage to get into one of the most crowded Zionist areas in the city of Jerusalem?

At 3 am the morning after Zainab's martyrdom-seeking operation, two trucks full of Israeli soldiers came to her house, showed Zainab's family a photograph of her severed head at the site of explosion, asked what room was hers, and blew that room up. It demolished the house where she and her aunt's family lived. Her uncle, Mustafa Shinawi approved of her suicide operation, saying, "Every Palestinian finds his own suitable way to protest the Israeli oppression."

"Suicide Bomber Zainab Abu Salem; Her head separated from her pure body, and her Ra'ala [Muslim headscarf] remains to decorate [her face]. Her place is in Paradise, where in the highest heavens, Zainab ... sister [who has been raised to the level] of men."

[English translation of the Arabic text in the Hamās children's newspaper Alfatah of September 22, 2004, in praise of 18 year-old martyr who was children's television presenter, Zainab Ali Issa Abu Salem]

A special note on Martyr Dalal Al-Mughrabi

Date of Martyrdom: 11th March, 1978

"Point your guns in only one direction- your enemy - Israel," urged Martyr Dalal Al Mughrabi in her final wish just before she laid down her life for the liberation of her occupied homeland, Palestine.

Martyr Dalal Al-Mughrabi was the first female commander in the history of the struggle of the Palestinian nation against the Zionist aggressors. She became a legend of courage and a symbol of resistance and martyrdom for the Palestinian nation for many years.

Martyr Dalal was born in the refugee camp of Sābra in Lebanon in 1958. She had never seen her homeland until the moment of her martyrdom. While having only 20 years of age, she trained and led 12 youths for carrying out one of the most audacious martyrdom-seeking operations against the Zionist army 30 years ago.

On the 11th of March 1978, Dalal, along with her group, managed to break into the Lebanese-Israeli border to the coastal plain near Tel Aviv using rubber dinghy boats. She and her group of resistance fighters destroyed the boats the moment they reached the coast. It was a unique one-way trip, as they had returned to their occupied homeland to stay or to die as martyrs.

Ehud Barak shamelessly dragging the dead body of Martyr Dalal Al-Mughrabi in front of international press photographers.

They then hijacked an Israeli military bus and took its passengers, the 83 Zionist soldiers, as hostages after driving the bus along the coastal highway to the colony of Herzliya, where a nine-hour battle took place between them and a special team of Israeli military forces, led by Ehud Barak, who later became Israel's prime minister and present defense minister. The aim of martyr Dalal and her group was to put pressure on the Zionist regime to release the Palestinians imprisoned in the Israeli jails.

Finally, this brave group, after inflicting much damage on the Israeli forces, was martyred on the highway between Tel Aviv and Haifa. This military operation was so important for Israel that Barak dragged the corpse of this courageous martyr in front of the press photographers and took photos to proudly show himself as victorious.

In July 2008, the bodies of Martyr Al-Mughrabi and her martyred group members were released from the Zionists army possession and returned to Palestine in a prisoner and bodies swap deal between Hizbollah and the Zionist regime.

A woman holds a photo of Martyr Dalal al-Mughrabi as a convoy carrying her body passes by on Beirut's airport road July 17, 2008.

After Dalal's martyrdom, this brave lady's mother said that she preferred that her daughter's body be buried in Palestine.

Three decades after her death, Dalal is still seen by Palestinians and Arabs as a hero and an outstanding fighter. In a message that she had sent shortly before her martyrdom, Dalal appealed during the last gasp of her life to the Palestinians to point their guns to their common enemy - Israel, and not to get involved in internal fighting.

She inspired thousands of young Palestinian and Lebanese women to follow in her footsteps, such as Sana Muhaidali[48], Loula Abboud[49], Wafa Al-Idrees, Ayat Al-Akhras and Hanādi Jarādāt among others.

According to her mother, who was speaking in a TV interview, "Dalal will never be forgotten as she will remain an admirable symbol of the Palestinian women's struggle and an example to be emulated by young Palestinian men and women who will pursue the armed struggle until the liberation of Palestine."

---

[48]Sana'a Mehaidli was a member of the Syrian Social Nationalist Party. In April 1985, at the age of 16 she carried out a martyrdom seeking operation in Jezzin, South Lebanon near an Israeli convoy, killing two Zionist soldiers and injuring others. She is popularly known as 'Bride of South'.

[49] Loula Abboud was a 19 year old Palestinian member of Lebanese Communist Party. On 20th April 1985, she shot at Zionist soldiers in Aoun Village in Lebanon and then detonated explosive device killing 1 soldier.

Epilogue

A curious mind asks a simple question: what motivated these young, educated and enlightened ladies to sacrifice their lives and give up all the pleasures of this world?

Offering one's life in the way of God is not something new. It has a long history. In Islam, it is a noble way of returning from this transient world to the eternal abode. A martyr makes this choice because of the love of God and duty to fulfill a noble cause towards oppressed fellow human beings and feels proud and satisfied with this lofty choice. A martyr is a passenger to heaven from this materialistic world – because his / her aim is divine.

When these noble daughters of olive gave their lives in the way of God, it made this world a hell for the Zionist Occupiers, as if the fire of God's anger fell down on their heads. These honorable and courageous ladies remind us of the brave and fearless men and women in the time of Prophet of God (s) and His grandson Imam Hussain (a).

There is another side of these honorable queens of paradise – and that is their tender heart and pure sincere love for the fellow human beings around them, their pain for oppressed men and humiliated women and innocent murdered children, their deeply anguished spirit that feels the unbearable hardships every day, the loss of the loved ones among Palestinian families, the cries of orphans, widows, weak and the old, aftermath of destructions of homes, massacres, tortures, kidnappings and detentions, crippled daily life, denial of basic rights and justice, international silence and the lack of UN action for their rights, open blatant support of the US and European governments for the Zionist regime and silence of other major powers in face of all the horrific Zionist crimes.

This noble way of martyrdom among the Palestinian Daughters of Olive is a golden era in the history of Palestine and modern world politics. It is certainly an eye opener for a conscious, unbiased, educated, freedom-lover human being, irrespective of religion, race, geographic boundaries and political affiliations. It certainly heralds the future of Palestine, that it will be liberated from the clutches of the merciless Zionist killers and oppressors.

Soon the world will witness that the material and political support of US and its allies for the Zionist regime will not be able to prevent the liberation of Palestine, punishment of the Zionist criminals and return of millions of refugees to their homeland. This is because so many martyrs gave their lives in this path, especially the Daughters of Olive, who gave their lives at the prime of their youth and gave their pure bodies and souls in God's way and so God will certainly bring victory for the sake of fulfillment of their dear wish – the liberation of Palestine - sooner or later. *InshaAllah*.

Index